Rose Martin is Senior Lecturer in Dance Studies, National Institute of Creative Arts, University of Auckland. A former dancer with the Royal New Zealand Ballet, her research interests include international education in dance, cross-cultural conceptualisations of the dancing body, dance and identity and dance in transnational contexts. She is the author of *Women, Dance and Revolution* (I.B.Tauris, 2015).

Eeva Anttila is Professor of Dance Pedagogy, Theatre Academy of University of the Arts Helsinki, Finland. Her research interests include dialogical and critical dance pedagogy, embodied learning, embodied knowledge and practice-based/artistic research methods. She served as the Chair of Dance and the Child International (2009–12), is co-editor of the *International Journal of Education in the Arts*, and is member of the editorial board of the *Nordic Journal of Dance: Practice, Education, and Research*.

TALKING DANCE

SERIES EDITORS: Nicholas Rowe and Ralph Buck, University of Auckland

The Talking Dance series presents the voices of people who dance in diverse communities, from village halls to metropolitan theatres. The humorous and poignant anecdotes reveal the challenges they face, the experiences they celebrate and the untold ways in which dance connects with their lives. Through their very personal journeys, the series promotes the socio-political relevance of dance in societies around the globe, and helps to deconstruct some of the restrictive parameters surrounding what it is to dance.

Published and forthcoming in the series:

Talking Dance: Contemporary Histories from the Southern Mediterranean by Nicholas Rowe, Ralph Buck and Rose Martin

Talking Dance: Contemporary Histories from the South China Sea by Nicholas Rowe and Ralph Buck with Toni Shapiro-Phim

Dance, Diversity and Difference: Performance and Identity Politics in Northern Europe and the Baltic by Rose Martin with Eeva Anttila

Talking Dance: Contemporary Histories from the South Pacific by Nicholas Rowe and Ralph Buck

Dance, Diversity and Difference

Performance and Identity Politics in Northern Europe and the Baltic

Rose Martin with Eeva Anttila

methuen | drama
LONDON · NEW YORK · OXFORD · NEW DELHI · SYDNEY

METHUEN DRAMA
Bloomsbury Publishing Plc
50 Bedford Square, London, WC1B 3DP, UK
1385 Broadway, New York, NY 10018, USA
29 Earlsfort Terrace, Dublin 2, Ireland

BLOOMSBURY, METHUEN DRAMA and the Methuen Drama logo are trademarks of Bloomsbury Publishing Plc

First published in Great Britain by I.B. Tauris 2018
This paperback edition published by Methuen Drama 2021

Copyright © Rose Martin, 2018, 2021

Rose Martin has asserted her right under the Copyright, Designs and Patents Act, 1988, to be identified as author of this work.

For legal purposes the Acknowledgements on pp. xi–xii constitute an extension of this copyright page.

Cover design by Ian ross www.ianrossdesigner.com
Cover image: Gosia Mielech, Poznań: We sometimes forget to enjoy dancing. Photo by Katarzyna Machniewicz

All rights reserved. No part of this publication may be reproduced or transmitted in any form or by any means, electronic or mechanical, including photocopying, recording, or any information storage or retrieval system, without prior permission in writing from the publishers.

Bloomsbury Publishing Plc does not have any control over, or responsibility for, any third-party websites referred to or in this book. All internet addresses given in this book were correct at the time of going to press. The author and publisher regret any inconvenience caused if addresses have changed or sites have ceased to exist, but can accept no responsibility for any such changes.

A catalogue record for this book is available from the British Library.

A catalog record for this book is available from the Library of Congress.

ISBN: HB: 978-1-7845-3979-5
PB: 978-1-3502-1088-2
ePDF: 978-1-7867-3243-9
eBook: 978-1-786-72243-0

Series: Talking Dance

Typeset by Riverside Publishing Solutions, Salisbury, SP4 6NQ
Printed and bound in Great Britain

To find out more about our authors and books visit www.bloomsbury.com and sign up for our newsletters.

For Sebastian Jo, and the many adventures ahead of you

Contents

Illustrations ix
Colour plates x
Acknowledgements xi
Series preface xiii

Introduction 1
Rose Martin and Eeva Anttila

1 Beginnings 19
2 Learning 40
3 Making 61
4 Performing 76
5 Teaching and teachers 101
6 Family, relationships and meetings 122
7 Heritage and history 137
8 Change and turning points 150
9 Travelling 162
10 Futures, challenges and questions 175

List of interviewees 185
List of references 188
Glossary 191
Notes 193
Index 194

Illustrations

Where possible images of interviewees correspond with their longer narratives. There are instances where the images shared are of different interviewees, however the photo captions included with these photos relate to the chapter.

The Baltic Sea, by Sholto Buck	xvi
The Baltic Sea, by Sholto Buck	17
Maija Rantanen, photo by Sara Estlander	20
Tony Antanas Ceponis, photo courtesy of Tony Antanas Ceponis	26
Modjgan Hashemian, photo courtesy of Modjgan Hashemian	29
Rash Sensei, photo courtesy of La Folie Crew	30
Piotr Zalipski, photo by K. Wojciewski	31
Anna Paś, photo by K. Wojciewski	37
Marija Kaklauskaite, photo courtesy of Marija Kaklauskaite	42
Maija Rantanen, photo by Sara Estlander	44
Njara Rasolo, photo courtesy of Njara Rasolo	45
Vytis Jankauskas, photo by Gediminas Jacikevicius	47
Vytis Jankauskas, photo courtesy of Vytis Jankauskas	48
Tony Antanas Ceponis, photo courtesy of Tony Antanas Ceponis	50
Vitaly Kim, photo courtesy of STAGE Company	57
Volker Eisenach, photo by Paul Lardon	62
Rash Sensei, photo courtesy of La Folie Crew	64
Gosia Mielech, photo by M. Zakrzewski	65
Tony Antanas Ceponis, photo courtesy of Tony Antanas Ceponis	69
Modjgan Hashemian, photo courtesy of Modjgan Hashemian	77
Anamet Magven, photo by Sameena Safiruddin	80
Marija Kaklauskaite, photo courtesy of Marija Kaklauskaite	84
Magdalena Zalipska, photo by K. Wojciewski	85
Anna Paś, photo by K. Wojciewski	87
Rash Sensei, photo courtesy of La Folie Crew	88
Maija Rantanen, photo by Sara Estlander	90
Moa Westerlund, photo courtesy of Moa Westerlund	91
Özen Erdinc, photo courtesy of Özen Erdinc	97
Vitaly Kim, photo courtesy of STAGE Company	102
Gosia Mielech, photo by Andrzej Janikowski	105

Vytis Jankauskas, photo by Dimitrij Matvejev	106
Rash Sensei, photo courtesy of La Folie Crew	108
Anamet Magven, photo courtesy of INSP!media	109
Volker Eisenach, photo by Alexandra Huebner	112
Alexa Wilson, photo by Jose G Cano	116
Alexa Wilson, photo by Jose G Cano	123
Modjgan Hashemian, photo courtesy of Modjgan Hashemian	128
Susanne Frederiksen, photo courtesy of Danish Parkinsonunion, photo by Nicola Fasano	129
Krysztof Fijak, photo by K. Wojciewski	132
Laura Lohi, photo courtesy of Laura Lohi	135
Uldim Steinam, photo courtesy of Uldim Steinam	141
Magdalena Zalipska, photo by K. Wojciewski	143
Volker Eisenach, photo by Paul Landon	147
Katerina Urbanovich, photo courtesy of STAGE Company	148
Modjgan Hashemian, photo courtesy of Modjgan Hashemian	151
Edmundus Zicka, photo courtesy of Edmundus Zicka	152
Piotr Zalipski, photo by K. Wojciewski	158
Rash Sensei, photo courtesy of La Folie Crew	160
Alexa Wilson, photo by Lydia Bittner-Baird	164
Vitaly Kim, photo courtesy of STAGE Company	165
Gosia Mielech, photo courtesy of Gosia Mielech	166
Veera Lamberg, photo courtesy of Veera Lamberg	169
Rash Sensei, photo courtesy of La Folie Crew	177
Gosia Mielech, photo by Katarzyna Machniewicz	178
Oxana Bellamy, photo courtesy of Oxana Bellamy	183
The Baltic Sea, by Sholto Buck	184

Colour plates

Tony Antanas Ceponis, photo courtesy of Tony Antanas Ceponis
Wioletta Milczuk, photo by K. Wojciewski
Majia Rantanen, photo by Sara Estlander
Piotr Zalipski, photo by K. Wojciewski
Laura Lohi, photo courtesy of Laura Lohi
Anamet Magven, photo courtesy of INSP! Media
Gosia Mielech, photo by M. Zakrzewski
Veera Lamberg, photo courtesy of Veera Lamberg
Gosia Mielech, photo courtesy of Gosia Mielech
Marija Kaklauskaite, photo courtesy of Marija Kaklauskaite
Modjgan Hashemian, photo courtesy of Modjgan Hashemian
Rash Sensei, photo courtesy of La Folie Crew

Acknowledgements

The *Talking Dance* books are only possible through the kindness, openness and generosity of the interviewees who share their stories within the following pages. Each person who gave an interview did it with warmth, honesty and a passion for sustaining and extending dance in some way. In any project that involves much planning, travel and along the way negotiation of languages, customs and cultures, specific people provide extra support and guidance. Often these people emerge throughout the journey, and reveal just how generous people can really be. They include: Maija Rantanen for connections in Helsinki; Olga Potapova for assisting with St Petersburg; Maria Nurmela for sharing connections in Sweden; Professor Charlotte Svendler-Nielsen for providing Copenhagen contacts; Iwona Wojnicka for translation, contacts and incredible hospitality in Warsaw; Iluta Goba for going above and beyond with introductions and translation in Riga; Jo Parkes for providing connections and sharing her work; Modjgan Hashemian for the inspiration and connections that extended well beyond the Baltic; Vita Khlopova for taking the time to travel from Moscow to have a long lunch; Inna Kransnoper for sharing contacts; Maarja Tonisson for Estonian connections; Leyya Tawil for introductions to St Petersburg friends; and Katerina Urbanovich for her translation work in St Petersburg. The assistance from University of Auckland Dance Studies postgraduate students in conducting Skype interviews and transcribing has also been invaluable, thank you to Amelia Chong and Kendall Jones for their work on this, and to Sholto Buck for his work on the maps included in the book.

The University of Auckland, through the Faculty Research and Development Fund, has kindly supported this research. We are ever grateful for the encouragement from Creative Arts and Industries Dean, Professor Diane Brand, and Head of Dance Studies, Associate Professor Ralph Buck, to continue to pursue this project. This research has also been undertaken as part of the

ArtsEqual Project funded by the Academy of Finland's Strategic Research Council from its Equality in Society Programme (project no. 293199).

Finally we would like to thank our colleagues, families and friends for their unwavering care throughout this journey of research and writing. The months of travel and the months of persevering with writing 'lock-down' is no easy task. Only through the support offered by those we love could we achieve this publication.

Series preface

Connected and disconnected
Nicholas Rowe and Ralph Buck

It was an unusually warm winter evening as we crossed the curving Millennium Bridge over the Tyne to Gateshead, reaching a virtual game-zone on the south bank. A 20-metre chunk of pavement had casually transformed into an interactive digital playing field. Encircled by movement sensors, colourful video images projected on the ground and shifted in response to our pathways across the space. Internet technology allowed our moving bodies to spontaneously challenge an unknown team somewhere else in the world.

We played.

We lost.

Panting from the unexpected exertion and pulling our jackets back on, we considered the wonders of technology that had allowed this brief, highly physical, international exchange. We moved on to the conference dinner, intrigued but bewildered as to who the other players might have been and how they had moved so well. Technology had very effectively connected and disconnected us, making it hard to celebrate the victory of our unknown playmates.

It was December 2009, and we were in Newcastle, UK, for the *World Alliance for Arts Education Global Summit*. With 11 dance educators among 46 educators in music, fine arts and drama from around the world, we were collectively drafting a policy document that would ultimately inform UNESCO's policy on Arts Education, which was ratified in Paris in 2011. This policy document identified imperatives for researching, networking and advocating arts education, so that artistic ways-of-knowing might remain central to learning in the twenty-first century, across the globe.

One of the challenges of the Summit was to gain global representation. Gathered in reflexive discussion around tables in Newcastle's Dance City studios, the prevailing languages indicated how hard this was to achieve. Financial restrictions meant that representation from the Majority World, or non-OECD countries, was not in proportion to the populations of those regions. Arts educators who were participating in the Summit from Africa, Asia, the Pacific, Central and South America also identified that, due to limited local networks and documentation, their own ability to represent the diverse aspirations and needs of these vast regions was particularly restricted.

One of the recommendations of the Newcastle Summit that was embraced in the UNESCO Seoul Agenda Policy was to 'Stimulate exchange between research and practice in arts education' (UNESCO, 2011).

Key action items as stated in the Seoul Agenda include:
- 2.c (i) Support arts education theory and research globally and link theory research and practice.
- 3.c (ii) Foster and exchange knowledge and understanding of diverse cultural and artistic expressions.

The *Talking Dance* series that this book is part of is therefore one answer to that call. These pages capture a discussion on dance practices that might prompt further research, and ultimately diversify contemporary global understandings of dance. Our focus is on regions of the world in which dance practices are currently under-documented, using research methods that might foster cultural autonomy and voice.

The twenty-first century offers unprecedented opportunities to physically engage with people in remote parts of the world, as our spontaneous digital dance by the banks of the Tyne affirmed. Advanced technology does not, however, ultimately guarantee that we value, learn from, tolerate and ultimately celebrate others at a distance.

Deconstructing and co-constructing impressions of self and other

Intercultural research and representation can be contentious. For several centuries, Western literary and artistic impressions of 'the Orient' have predominantly used a lens that sought to distinguish the Orient from the Occident. Emphasising the exotic and the intransigence of Africa and Asian cultures, such Orientalist representations can be seen justifying the subjugation of non-European people within European colonial empires (Said, 1978).

In adopting a post-Orientalist lens (Prakash, 1990), this book series maintains an intercultural curiosity, yet seeks to deconstruct many of the legacies of Orientalism. This starts with a challenge to contemporary cultural and political literature that would seek to identify differences between the West and the Rest (Huntington, 1997; Lewis, 2002). We have sought to evidence the hybrid nature of contemporary cultures around the world (Bhabha, 1994), and challenge attempts to generalise about cultural difference.

Our post-nationalist view has similarly sought to consider how dance might deconstruct the imagined communities of nationalism and ethnicity (Anderson, 1991). Dance has played a central role in the construction of national and ethnic identities, particularly through the performance of folklore (Shay, 1999). This process has generally involved the invention of traditions (Hobsbawm and Ranger, 1983), the appropriation of cultural items, and the construction of static, often polemic, cultural canons (Chatterjee, 1993). Such heritage manifestos have reflected the patriarchal political orders among the political leadership that instituted them, and inevitably the dance practices of divergent, disempowered and minority voices were written and danced out of history. We have therefore sought voices that do not always find a place within such national histories.

Our post-colonial view (Asad, 1973; Tuhiwai Smith, 1999) has also sought to co-construct meanings of dance with local dance practitioners, to provoke and then feed back local reflections on dance. Within the Southern Mediterranean, this has involved engaging in long-term partnerships, discussing and disseminating our findings through ongoing symposiums, conferences and dance education projects in the region.

The central aim of *Talking Dance* is therefore to evidence the diversity and dynamism of dance in distinct regions of the world, thus far documenting experiences from the Southern Mediterranean, South China Sea and Baltic Sea. It seeks to illustrate that there are many different pathways into dance, ways of learning dance, of being accepted into dance professions, of creating dance, of performing dance, of watching dance, of organising dance events; that dance has diverse connections with families, societies, governments, the economy, the past and the future; that the actual experiences of dance practitioners are fascinating, are culturally relevant and challenge any attempt to stereotype, define or otherwise distinguish what it means to dance around the world.

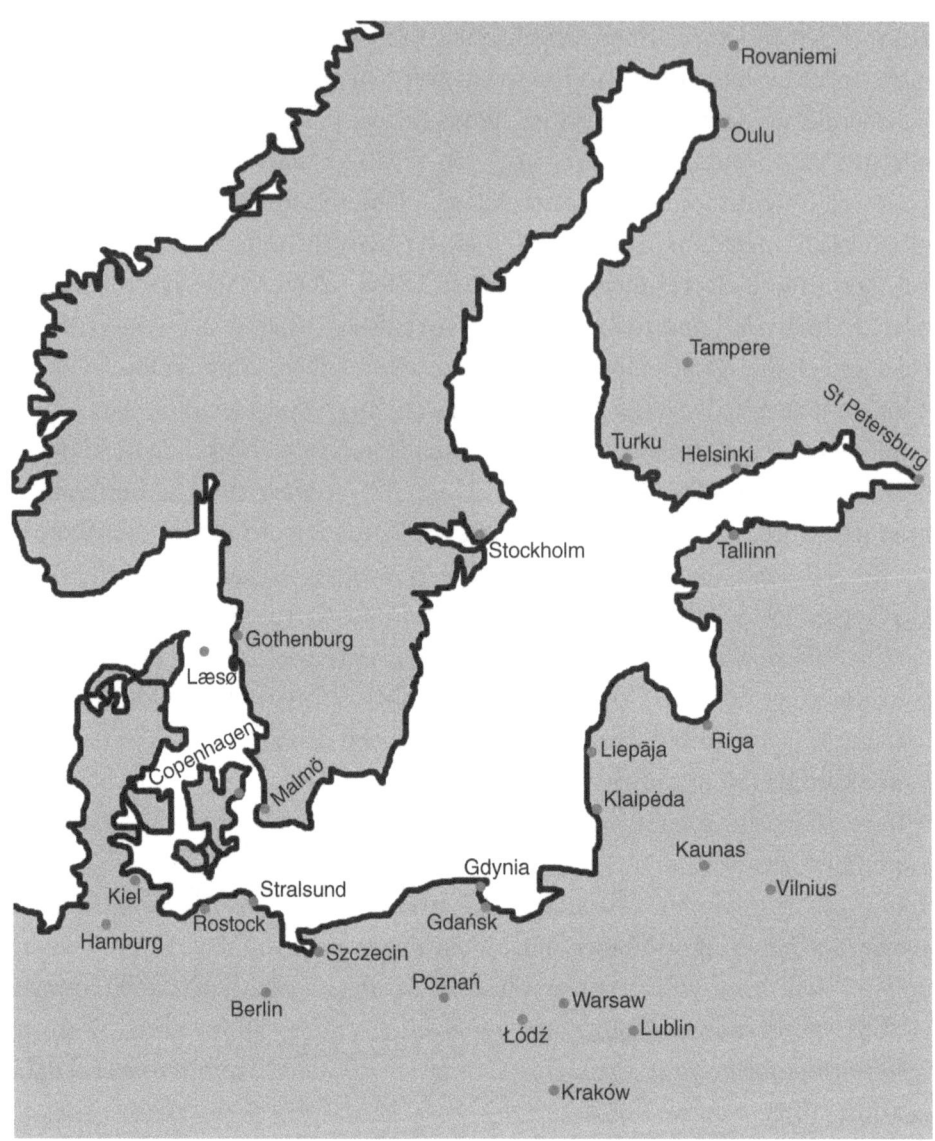

The Baltic Sea

Introduction

'I am sorry, I don't speak German'
Rose Martin

I was lost. Again.
I was running late. Again.

My walk turned into a jog as I made a second lap of the Berlin Hauptbahnhof looking for the S-Bahn I needed to take to get to Westkreuz. I stopped under one of the large 'arrivals' and 'departures' boards, to check to see if anything on the boards might provide a clue to where I needed to be. I squinted at the fuzzy writing, wishing I had brought my glasses with me. So focused on trying to read I barely noticed the older man standing next to me inch closer to my side. Only when he said 'entschuldigung' did I see that he was there and holding a piece of paper in his hand outstretched towards me. On the paper was an address scrawled in red pen. I looked at the man, and saw that behind him stood a woman and two teenage children, a boy and a girl. As I began to open my mouth to say 'I'm sorry, I don't speak German', the teenage boy who would have been no older than 16 stepped next to the man, who I could only assume was his father, and said in a thick Levantine accent, 'no Deutsch…'. Things began to make sense. I asked, 'hal tatakallam Alearabia?' Their eyes widened looking both genuinely shocked and ecstatically happy. 'Alearabia!' the boy said enthusiastically. The boy explained that they were looking for the train to Neukölln. Together in a mixture of English, Arabic and a smattering of German, and enlisting the help from those around us, we found their platform.

I waited with them for the train to arrive and they told me snippets of their story, first of all how they had only been in Berlin for a short time, and that their home was Aleppo. I said that I had visited Aleppo just before the War started in 2011, and that allowed us to bond even further. The daughter asked me, 'did you go to the famous ice cream shop in the souk? It was the best!' As the train approached the platform the family thanked me multiple times, the mother took my hand in hers saying 'shukran jazilaan' before they all headed off into the distance on the platform.

I looked at the time on my phone, I was going to be exceptionally late to my first interview in Berlin.

The countries surrounding the Baltic Sea are on a precipice of change, upheaval or some might even say crisis. The cities and towns in the Baltic region are not alone, the entire continent of Europe has recently been unsettled, especially with the arrival of more than 1 million migrants in 2015 and many more in 2016, providing the largest inflow of people to the continent since World War II. Civil wars, uprisings, dictatorships and the terror of groups such as the Islamic State have forced an unprecedented number of people around the world to leave their homes and seek refuge in safer locations. While some countries (such as Jordan or Turkey) bear a mammoth share of refugees, greater numbers than ever before are turning to Europe, and particularly the European Union, in hope of a life in peace and relative prosperity. The 'right to seek and to enjoy in other countries asylum from persecution' is enshrined in the Universal Declaration of Human Rights of 1948, and implies that people seeking shelter in new locations are often travelling under excruciating conditions and carrying traumatised pasts (Razum and Bozorgmehr, 2015). Often those arriving in a new country as refugees or asylum seekers are facing new languages, customs, cultures and social expectations, with little to no financial support, secure employment or family networks. While individuals are largely showing compassion and kindness to those arriving in Europe, Europe's leaders continue to play to their own agendas and some groups are hostile to these new arrivals.

These new migrations appear to be challenging Europe's resilience. Border controls are tightening across the continent, and the crisis has exposed some strikingly concerning attitudes, including a worrying level of prejudice, especially from far-right ultra nationalist organisations.[1] Tense inter-relationships between states, groups of people and notions of who 'belongs' where have emerged. Across the region, fears over terrorism have been expressed, along with scepticism over the authenticity of refugees' claims to be fleeing war, as well as outright racism and xenophobia towards those who are deemed to be 'non-European'. It could be said that there is a substantial amount of fear around the changes that are occurring in the region, and concern around how these changes might be negotiated.

It is easy to feel untouched by the problems of others when dealing with large-scale issues such as the refugee crisis in Europe. It may seem overwhelming to consider how we might create a more tolerant, equitable and peaceful world within such conditions. There is the potential that individuals do not feel strongly enough that they are part of a global community, part of a larger collective 'we'. This needs to change. Providing access to facts and figures can leave people feeling bewildered and disconnected, not necessarily empowered and poised for action. This is where the stories shared within the *Talking Dance* books can make a difference. The stories and reflections on dance as both life and art might not immediately show people what to do to solve a situation, but they do have the potential to connect with the senses, emotions, mind and body. A rich descriptive and evocative story can make the world felt, and this felt feeling may spur thinking, engagement, and even action. Through bringing people together to share and discuss – either face-to-face, virtually or vicariously – there is the potential to foster awareness, and perhaps in turn tolerance, acceptance and celebration of differences.

Why dance in the Baltic region?
Eeva Anttila

I have lived most of my life by the shores of the Baltic Sea. My first home was in Vaskiluoto, an island by the small Finnish coastal city of Vaasa, connected to the city by a bridge. There, I used to play by the harbour with my friends, sneaking into the cruise ships, sometimes taking the ship over to Umeå or Sundsvall with my family.

My enduring love for dance was ignited during my childhood years in Vaasa, where my older sister took ballet classes when I was still too young for it. The ballet school closed its doors before I was old enough to take classes, but having witnessed the beautiful costumes and recitals that sparked my imagination and desire for performing, nothing would stop me from pursuing dance later in my life. It was when my family and I moved to another harbour town, Kotka, that I was able to fulfil my dancing dreams. An industrial town rich in local culture, life in Kotka is influenced by the Baltic Sea in so many ways. Each summer the Kotka Maritime Festival, arranged almost every summer since 1962, attracts thousands of visitors to the city, with many arriving by boats. This festival connects maritime activities with cultural events such as a sailor song contest and a children's culture festival. The children's programme was initiated in 1983, and this event is considered the official commencement of the children's culture activities of the city. The programme also included a local production of an outdoor children's opera *Mörköooppera* ('Ghost opera' – that has absolutely nothing to do with 'Phantom opera'). I had the privilege to be in charge of the choreography, working with children from local schools, and adult volunteers who formed the core of the performing ensemble. Witnessing the joy and excitement of the children, as well as the warm reception of this production by the audience and the city, strengthened my commitment to keep working in the area of children's culture and performing arts.

Dancing, acting and playing the piano filled my youth during the long cold winter months, while the white night summers were quite the opposite, and I was occupied with swimming, boating and fishing, either at our family's summer cottage in Ravijoki, close to the Russian border, or at my best friend Katriina's summer house on the southernmost inhabited island of Finland, Utö. I remember in these locations that the water was clear, the seaweed was bright green and soft, and the sea was still healthy. Nowadays things are different. During summer, some areas of the Baltic Sea turn into disgusting porridge-like waters, with poisonous blue-green algae. Many artists are active in the Baltic Sea Project that supports efforts to create a healthier Baltic Sea by, for example, raising public awareness about the state of the Baltic Sea. I see that this reflects the importance of the Baltic Sea to artists and many other inhabitants who love this enclosed and endangered sea, as a continuous source of inspiration and recuperation.

Although all the shores of the Baltic Sea that are represented in this book are familiar to me from one viewpoint or another – from the deck of a cruise ship, from biking and hiking around the islands, from driving around and through the Baltic countries, and from multiple visits with dancing colleagues in most Baltic countries – I look at the Baltic Sea and dance around the region from my home location of Helsinki, Finland. Finland is a unique country in between the East and the West, geographically, historically, politically and culturally. Cultural influences, both in the form of folk dance and dance art, from Central Europe add to our diverse background in art and dance. However, it seems to me that our relationship to embodied interaction and bodily expression is controversial and complicated. On one hand, our folk dances, like those of other Nordic and North European countries, reflect formal and 'upright' – both literally and metaphorically – relationships to body movement and expressivity, where movement of the torso is very limited, and where touching others, especially the other gender, is restricted because of moral and religious beliefs. On the other hand, social dancing at special dance halls is a highly popular activity among all social classes, ages and backgrounds. Social dance events and dance halls built especially for this purpose can be found everywhere in Finland. During the light summer nights, dancing takes place in half open halls and is accompanied by live popular music, and during dark winter months dance events are arranged in restaurants, senior centres, even at the National Opera House, and thousands of couples take part.

Another unique phenomenon is the Finnish tango. Every July, the centre of Seinäjoki, a town of about 60,000 inhabitants in central Finland, becomes transformed into a vast dance hall where thousands of ordinary people gather to dance tango for several days. They dance to tango tunes performed by Finnish popular musicians, take tango lessons and participate in contests, all day and night. The tango, in its special Finnish style and character, expresses the passion and melancholy that Finns seem to have a strong connection to. Seinäjoki is the regional centre of South Ostrobothnia, situated very close to Vaasa where I was born, and even closer to my family roots. This area is largely rural, very flat and the people are known for their stubborn character, and their need for independence and personal space. For me, it is a small wonder how Seinäjoki has become the centre of an inclusive dancing event that connects thousands of people who spend most of the year working in their farms or small businesses. The Seinäjoki tango festival is, for me, an icon of the transformative power of dance.

In Helena Saarikoski's (2014) book *Back then we danced the tango: Tales by dance folks from the 1900s*, the many shades and meanings that tango and other social dance forms have had for ordinary Finns are explored. The book is a collection of narratives selected by Saarikoski from an archive based on an open writing contest held in 1991. Exploring these stories, tango seems to hold a special status. One person writes, 'when tango came to the dance halls, the ones who could dance it were admired' (Saarikoski, p.61). Another writer says that, 'when tango was played, I had to go and dance and get close to a boy' (p.190). The account by which the book got its name is as follows:

> Back then we danced the tango! ... The tango was the most popular dance. There was the beginning and ending waltz, but otherwise we danced the tango.
>
> (Saarikoski, p.215)

I believe the long, white summer nights after long and dark winter months have shaped the dance cultures around the Baltic Sea. A strong connection to nature and artistic inspiration from nature characterises Nordic art, including dance. An example of this is the work of the Swedish pioneer of children's dance, Eva Dahlgren (1915–2008), who was known for her dance events in the hills of northern Sweden. Also, huge outdoor folk dance festivals are an important community-building force in the Baltic countries, especially Estonia, Latvia and Lithuania. In addition to classical ballet, folk dance is still the most important form of dance in education in these countries. Creative, more individualistic or child-centred approaches to dance and dance education, imports from the Anglo–American world, seem to gain more interest slowly but steadily across the region.

The same development began about 30 years ago in Finland, when a national organisation for children's dance was established soon after the first Finnish dance educators became involved in daCi (dance and the Child international). With the Finnish tradition of women's gymnastics, which had strong influences from modern dance pioneers (most notably Maggie Gripenberg, who studied modern dance and rhythmics in Central Europe during early 1900s), the ground for creative dance was fertile. The eminent Russian ballet teacher Agrippina Vaganova still holds her steady grip on young ballet students studying at the Finnish National Ballet School today. Just a block away at the Theatre Academy at the University of the Arts Helsinki, contemporary dance students move in sync with their peers in Berlin.

Influences from the south, west and east of the Baltic region have merged into and on our dance stages, halls, streets and studios, with the Baltic Sea both separating and connecting cultures, ideas and people, it is a liquid passage that carries and bonds.

History of the Baltic region
Rose Martin and Eeva Anttila

The Baltic Sea (also called the Ostsee, Morze Bałtyckie, Bałtyk, Балтийское море, Østersøen, Östersjön, Baltijos jūra, Baltijas jūra, Läänemeri and Itämeri) has long been a region of exchange and encounter, and a location for military and economic interests (North, 2015). As a semi-enclosed inland sea situated in Northern Europe, it is considered an extension of the Atlantic Ocean, connected via the Kattegat Strait, Skagerrak Strait and the North

Sea. It extends northward from the south of Denmark to within a few degrees latitude of the Arctic Circle, separating the Scandinavian Peninsula from continental Europe. Aside from being called 'the Baltic', the Sea has two kinds of names. For those in Germany, Sweden, Denmark and Finland it is an eastern sea, and for those in Estonia and Latvia it is a western sea. For others in the region it is simply 'the Baltic', and there are differing theories of the origin of this name. A common idea is that the word Baltic emerged from the Latvian word balts or the Lithuanian word baltas, meaning white (Palmer, 2007; Voipio, 1981). Formed in a basin on top of the East European Craton millions of years after it consolidated, the Baltic Sea had several prehistoric stages before forming into the sea we encounter today. The Baltic Sea is generally brackish, poor in oxygen and with limited sea life (Jansson, 2003), with the exception being the Kattegat and the southwestern Baltic Sea that both have a rich biology and are well oxygenated. In the waters there are unique nuances, including the Baltic Sea anomaly, a 60-metre diameter circular rock-like formation on the floor of the northern Baltic Sea, at the centre of the Bothnian Sea. Discovered by a Swedish diving team in 2011, it was reported that the formation sits on a pillar and includes a structure similar in appearance to a staircase, leading to a dark hole. It is unclear what has led to the formation, and it has been suggested that the structure could be a World War II anti-submarine device, a battleship gun turret, sediment dropped by a fishing trawler or even a flying saucer.

The region itself is referred to in slightly different ways, depending on the combinations of countries included, and it is frequently acknowledged as the 'Baltic region' or the 'Baltic rim'. Frequently Latvia, Lithuania and Estonia are referred to as the Baltic States (Lane, Pabriks, Purs and Smith, 2013). With this in mind the definitions of what constitutes the Baltic region are multiple, with as many variations as there are map makers who have drawn the outlines of the Baltic Sea (Maciejewski, 2002). For this publication the decision was made to include countries that have shorelines along the Baltic Sea: Denmark, Estonia, Latvia, Finland, Germany, Lithuania, Poland, Russia and Sweden. Simultaneously, like the other *Talking Dance* books, this volume seeks to engage in a post-national dialogue, moving beyond nation states and borders. Therefore throughout the book the cities and towns of those who share their stories are included as identifiable information rather than using national labels. If an individual refers to a nation state in their story then it has remained within the narrative. However, a conscious decision has been made to allow those who were interviewed to articulate this themselves if they choose to do so, rather than imposing national labels on their practices or who they are as people.

Within the complexity of how the region is defined and described, is a turbulent and intricate history. In the period of the Roman Empire, the Baltic Sea was known as the Mare Suebicum or Mare Sarmaticum with literature from this time documenting the brackish and icy waters. During the Viking/ Norsemen age the Baltic emerged as a significant trade route, witnessing piracy, colonisation and long periods of conflict (Ferguson, 2009; Winroth, 2014). Over time, various countries surrounding the Baltic Sea have held the 'power' of and over these waters; there have been moments where the Sea has become a mass grave and periods where it has witnessed disastrous shipwrecks and maritime tragedies (Mack, 2013), the most recent maritime disaster being the sinking of the MS Estonia on 28 September 1994 as it travelled from Tallinn to Stockholm; 852 lives were lost and it is considered to be one of the worst maritime disasters in the twentieth century.

There have also been instances where these waters have flourished. From the Middle Ages to the late seventeenth century the Baltic was a vibrant cooperative cultural and economic zone (Maciejewski, 2002). However, power politics and tensions ensued, and within contemporary history of the Baltic the waters have by no means been smooth.

The Kingdom of Sweden took territorial control of much of the Baltic region during the seventeenth and early eighteenth centuries, until Russia, Saxony and Denmark began a concerted effort to reclaim territories (Palmer, 2007), with the waters of the Baltic allowing access to make claims over the surrounding lands. Over the eighteenth century the Russian Empire grew in power in the Baltic region, occupying Finland, controlling much of Poland and holding power in Latvia, Lithuania and Estonia until it was overthrown by the short-lived liberal February Revolution in 1917 (Trotsky and Eastman, 2008).

The events of World War II included the Baltic Sea campaigns in the Baltic Sea itself, its coastal regions and the Gulf of Finland, between the Axis and Allied[2] naval forces. The campaigns included surface and subsurface combat, aerial combat, amphibious landings, and provided support and transportation for the large-scale ground fighting that took place on the lands surrounding the Baltic. However, the most notable aspect of the Baltic Sea operations was the scale and size of mine warfare, particularly in the Gulf of Finland, the easternmost arm of the Baltic Sea (Davis, 2015). It has been documented that the warring parties placed over 60,000 naval mines and anti-sweep obstacles in this area, making the Gulf of Finland one of the most densely mined waters in the world (Maciejewski, 2002).

The East/West divide that was established following the end of World War II in 1945 led to further tensions and animosity across the Baltic Sea, most notably when Germany was split between the two global blocs of the East and West. Within this divide, the Eastern Bloc was understood as the group of communist states of Central and Eastern Europe, mainly the Soviet Union and the countries of the Warsaw Pact (Bunce, 1985). At this time the power of the USSR (Union of Soviet Socialist Republics) extended across around half of the countries bordering on the Baltic Sea, and the Soviet Union encouraged respect for Russian culture and actions. Through the hegemonic power asserted, Soviet hierarchies and processes in the Eastern Bloc were constructed (Davis, 2015).

Within the late 1980s tides began to turn, and the tensions that had rippled through the Baltic began to calm. A weakened Soviet Union cautiously stopped constraining and influencing the internal affairs of Eastern Bloc nations, and as the Soviet Union began to crumble (Stokes, 1993), numerous independence movements took place and the Eastern Bloc countries started to regain independence. Amid the breakup of the Soviet Union, revolutionary waves and uprisings took place, including the Revolutions in 1989/Autumn of Nations, The Barricades events in Latvia, and the Singing Revolution[3] in Latvia, Lithuania and Estonia (Ginkel, 2002; Thomson, 1992). Within these uprisings the arts became a powerful weapon of non-violent resistance to communist rule as the call for independence was made (Šmidchens, 2007, 2014). When the Soviet Union formally dissolved on 26 December 1991, the notion of a collective Baltic Sea region had to be re-imagined, with suggestions that this was the opportunity for the emergence of a new Baltic regional identity, not only in the post-USSR states, but within Northern Europe too (Mouritzen, 1993; Wæver, 1992). The Cold War era had resulted in a unity of the region stretching across the Iron Curtain that was impossible to sustain, and the dispansion of the Soviet Bloc has resulted in complex political ramification in post-Soviet Baltic locations (Latvia, Lithuania, (East) Germany, Poland and Estonia) (Sarotte, 2014).

In light of such upheavals the Nordic countries around the Baltic Sea – Finland, Sweden and Denmark – embarked on the development and commitment to a distinctly social-democratic set of internationalist values (Wæver, 1992), simultaneously Germany has been navigating through its reunification process (Pfeifer, Smolny and Wagner, 2016), and Poland, the

Baltic States and Russia have encountered a variety of post-Soviet Union reforms including privatisation and market and trade liberalisation (Hamm, King and Stuckler, 2012).

Multicultural and multilingual, the Baltic in the present day is a diverse region with a fluidity of space and borders in relation to the European Union groupings (Melnikas, 2008), yet still sustains sentiments of the past. Tensions surrounding the Baltic Sea have not dissipated, rather new challenges and contentions have emerged. For example, the Nord Stream offshore natural gas pipeline, which is in the process of being built from the Russian town of Vyborg across the Baltic Sea to Greifswald in Germany, has encountered much political controversy and opposition from various European leaders and environmental groups. Simultaneously, the increasing Russian military presence and activation around the Baltic has provided a cause for concern and questioning of what this might lead to. The diversity of the Baltic region is by no means unique to this part of the world, however within the current contemporary climate of a globalised world, with increasing mobility of people, identities, cultures and politics in the region (by choice or by force), it is ever increasing.

When walking through the streets of various Baltic cities it was clear that new communities, comprised of people from all over the world, were forming. With the arrival of new people, novel and diverse expectations, needs and values are brought to the fore. Communities are increasingly multifaceted, and this can be witnessed in the emergent demographic look and feel of the Baltic. Our present histories reveal varied perspectives that reflect diverse communities and politics. When exploring the past, present and future of a region no one history is adequate, or necessarily relevant. Stories, in all their multiplicity and diversity, are perhaps a better way to reveal examples of histories that are in tune with everyday realities. As societies in the Baltic region morph rapidly, history cannot remain in the pen and hand of one or more historians who hold a particular ideology and experience. Offering more people more ways to reveal the nuances of their lives is possibly an insightful way to reveal history, while also contemplating, questioning and proposing possible futures.

A globalised improvisational ethnography
Rose Martin

The train rocks melodically along the tracks between Warsaw and Poznań. I sit opposite a woman who looks like my grandmother. There is the same shape to her facial features, the same stature of barely reaching five feet tall, and eyes of a near identical dove-blue shade. The cramped compartment of carriage number 16 has a clammy heat to it; a heat wave has made this July day especially warm. Suitcases are perched precariously on rusty racks overhead, and shopping bags act as footrests. There is just the tiniest sliver of space to exit the compartment, and no one is moving anywhere, leaving me ample time to observe my grandmother's doppelgänger. She opens a packet of biscuits and offers me one. I feel strangely at home. We begin to talk and it is soon revealed that her good friend is a dance teacher in Warsaw. I mention how I am looking for more people to interview and she quickly scribbles down a name and phone number on a scrap of cardboard torn from the biscuit packet and hands it to me. She says, 'tell her Grażyna told you to call, I know she has some good stories to tell'.

Through each experience I have with ethnographic fieldwork the more that I see that it is improvisatory in nature (Cerwonka and Malkki, 2008). Like improvisation in dance, improvisation in ethnography often means that there is a structure, task or idea motivating actions, it is not entirely random, but within the frame created there are many possibilities about how events might unfold. Within the context of the *Talking Dance* books, multi-sited ethnography (Falzon, 2016; Marcus, 1995, 1998) is used as an interpretive way of knowing, with the research unfolding in real time and requiring a significant amount of thinking on one's feet. The processes of these ethnographic encounters reflect daily life, as R. Keith Sawyer (2000) articulates, 'everyday conversation is creatively improvised – there is no script that guides a conversation' (p. 149), and could be seen as a performative act in and of itself. Within this process there is a conscious shift away from representation and theorising, and more towards the *doing* of the research (Castañeda, 2006). The invisible theatre (Boal, 1985, 1992) of ethnography involves strategic provocation and an improvised dramatic script to trigger responses, engagement and exchange. These tactics and triggers within the fieldwork reveal that 'the performativity of fieldwork as ontological being [there in the field] cannot be separated from the doing of fieldwork as the gathering of data' (Castañeda, 2006, p.94).

I would often arrive in a new town or city with a few contacts in place and interviews scheduled. Some of these contacts were sought through colleagues, other interviewees, friends or friends of friends, and others I 'cold-called' after extensively searching for dance work in the region on the internet, through YouTube, websites, Instagram accounts and Facebook pages. It was always unknown how many people I might actually be able to meet in one place, and what stories they might tell me. It was a continual improvisation, from the moment I would ask someone to do an interview right through to when the voice recorder was turned off.

The improvisational nature of ethnography extends into the strategic and ethical choices that often have to be made instantaneously in the middle of an interview. There are moments when interviewees tell stories of the loss of a family member, or the connection to a past lover, an opportunity lost or an illness or injury that caused pain. I found I have had to become quickly attuned to the subtle signs of discomfort or sadness, and the moments to allow these to play out or the times to change direction with the conversation. The reality is that the ethnographer in the field is not perfect, with highly romanticised notions existing of being ever tolerant, sympathetic and open minded. There have been times in an interview where I have been bored, or frustrated or desperate to argue with the perspective being shared. Despite these imperfections throughout the research I aimed to develop situations where mutual trust, respect and understanding was fostered and there was a genuine exchange of thoughts, experiences and ideas (Heyl, 2001). There are times where I reflect on an interview for days after the event, considering how I might have approached things differently, critically examining my words and actions to try to understand how an alternative response might have been gained or if I did or said something different in the interview moment.

The *Talking Dance* books seek to explore the unique narrative of the individual, in all its messy, confusing, exciting chaos, and through this, actively challenge attempts to construct a regional collective identity of dance or dancers in any particular location, allowing national identities to be somewhat transcended. Within the book series we aim to share fragments of experiences, providing etchings of encounters, rather than offering summaries or synopses of the stories individuals have offered us. The fragments of dance selected to be included in this book are the moments of epiphany, the 'ah-ha' moments, turning points, transitions, revelations or moments that have been carved in the minds of those telling the story in a way that leaves an enduring impression. Often through the re-telling of experiences there were realisations about the present, and comments such as 'I had never really thought about that until now'. Within this research there is no intention to claim that the narratives shared by the interviewees are more 'authentic' than other methods of representation, neither do they sit outside of the socio-cultural contexts from which they have emerged. Instead, it is proposed that they provide snapshots of memories and reflections of particular times of individuals' lives, while acknowledging the inter-subjectivity of the inquiry and the multiple ways in which the events and experiences shared could be organised, viewed and interpreted.

Collectively, the interviewee and I create the conversation, and the conversation is informed by the particular time and place we are situated in (Connelly and Clandinin, 1990). Details as small as the coffee shop we might be meeting in, the time of day, what happened on the journey to arrive at our meeting and what might be happening afterwards can have a profound impact on the stories that are told, and how they are told. The length of each conversation varied depending on the individual, time and conversational flow. Sometimes narratives were built slowly over the course of a long conversation with a lot of talking and sharing of my own stories to encourage the interviewee along. There were other times when I would ask one question and the narrative unfolded in rhythmic waves, almost unprompted. The interviews were often conducted in English, and when translation was required I relied on local interpreters, all of whom were from the local dance communities.

It is not always easy to gain personal anecdotes from someone you may have only just met. Often people might be more inclined to share with you an opinion or a summative overview, rather than a tangible personal experience. My 'in' to a discussion where the space was opened for an anecdote to be revealed was often through the question 'Could you tell me about your earliest dancing memory?' Interviewees would then begin to share a moment along the lines of dancing in their dining room as a child, a first dance class, watching dance on television or moving in the school playground. As they shared the memory I would ask if they remembered the time of day, the temperature, what they were wearing, who else was there, how it felt kinaesthetically, if there was a particular smell or sound that they recall. These prompts would often take the memory further, digging deeper to extract more detail to allow the story to trickle out. Sometimes few prompts were needed and stories emerged with astounding detail, and my job was to simply sit back and listen.

Doing the research
Rose Martin

I woke up at 2.20a.m. with my heart racing, drenched in sweat and my breath trapped high up in my chest. Where was I? Tallinn? Helsinki? St Petersburg?

I had spent week eight 'on the road'. I had spent more weeks of the year living out of a suitcase than living at my 'home' in Auckland, New Zealand. I was tired. Not just the 'I need a nap and a coffee' sort of tired, but the 'I ache to my bones and can't see clearly' tired. I was travelling to a new location every few days, interviewing up to four people a day, and I was exhausted by continually meeting new people, finding new places, getting lost and being confused. It was like continual one-night stands, diving quickly into the most intimate details of someone's life story that they were willing to share and then making a swift exit out of the liaison. I pined for the familiar. I tried to calm my breathing by closing my eyes, and beginning to count slowly to five as I inhaled, and again to five as I exhaled. I felt my heart beat returning to a steady pace and my shoulders and chest relax. I opened my eyes and in the darkness could see the outline of the furniture in the room. I was quite certain I was in St Petersburg. However, I didn't trust myself and just to be sure I got out of bed, opened the plush curtains and looked outside. The lights of Nevsky Prospekt extended into the distance and the neon sign of a convenience store across the street flashed the words табак and водка intermittently. Hello St Petersburg, my new friend.

Work and life become one when engaging in fieldwork that takes you on long journeys; you embody the research in a way that is inescapable and consuming, and the multi-sited nature of research such as this requires continual reinvention, at each new city or town the 'game' begins again. Over the period the interviews for this book were gathered I travelled to nine countries, 16 cities, meeting with 65 interviewees who generously gave their time to sit with me and share their stories. While doing the research can have moments of being hectically busy, I have found that there is also a lot of time spent alone, wandering new cities, thinking and contemplating the new information and interactions encountered.

Fieldwork, for someone who is very much an outsider, yet appears (aesthetically anyway) to be an insider, is in stark contrast to some of the other fieldwork situations I have found myself in, namely when working on the *Talking Dance: Contemporary Histories from the Southern Mediterranean* book and subsequent research and publications in the 'Middle East'. As I walked through the streets of Warsaw looking for dance studios and cafes to meet interviewees, people would ask me for directions that I could not help them with, and words in swift Polish would tumble past me. The imagined sense of place and home I had could be because of the stories I was told since childhood, of my great-great-grandmother who was from Poland, and moved to New Zealand as an adventurous young woman. As I weaved my way around the Baltic, starting in Helsinki and concluding in St Petersburg, I noticed the moments of ease when I 'blended in' and the confused looks on faces as I started to speak and my New Zealand accent tumbled out. 'You don't speak Russian?' they would ask. With one shopkeeper following this up with, 'Are you sure?' Yes, I am quite sure.

Piecing it all together
Rose Martin and Eeva Anttila

The aim of the *Talking Dance* books is to share stories of dance, rather than specific dancers' stories. It intends to provide a montage of experiences, thoughts and encounters rather than profiles of dancers or dance companies in their entirety. Some stories are short, just a sentence or two. Others are longer and run for a page or more. The concept of allowing the stories to exist as a tableau has required balance in relation to offering the reader a sense of progression, yet at the same time providing the opportunity for each story to stand on its own and for the reader to interpret and analyse it in their own way.

Sifting and sorting through hundreds of hours of interview material is no easy task. The process of transcribing each interview takes much time, and then this transcription is returned to the interviewee for checking before the work begins of editing and sorting the material into the structure seen within this book. In all of the *Talking Dance* books certain themes are revealed during the interviews and through the stories that flow. Some of these themes appear to be the same within each book. Nearly everyone has a story about their dance beginnings, many have stories of teaching, learning, making and performing dance. Then there are themes that are unique and specific to the region. In the instance of the Baltic Sea the idea of change has emerged, change in directions, change of perceptions, change of landscape or change of socio-political terrain. These themes have shaped the structure of this book.

Many of the interviewees shared images of their work as dancers, teachers, choreographers or directors to be included in the book. These images were frequently provided from the interviewees' personal collections, some are professional images and others are informal shots snapped on an iPhone in the middle of a rehearsal. Some of the interviewees provided 20 images for us to choose from, others offered three or four, and some gave none. We did not have the intention of having an image for every interviewee; rather, it was the interviewee's choice about what they might include as a visual representation of their dance work alongside the text from their interview. Alongside the photographs sit short quotes extracted from the full interviews, sometimes these quotes are just a few words that can reveal a profound story.

As the reader delves into the following chapters it will be apparent that we have moved away from contextual analysis and meaning-making of the stories shared, with the intention of the interviewees' voices being at the fore, rather than ours as the researchers dominating discourses. For us, the stories that have emerged reveal a new way of understanding people and dance. The stories value experiences, offer insight and contribute to a shared history of dance within the Baltic region.

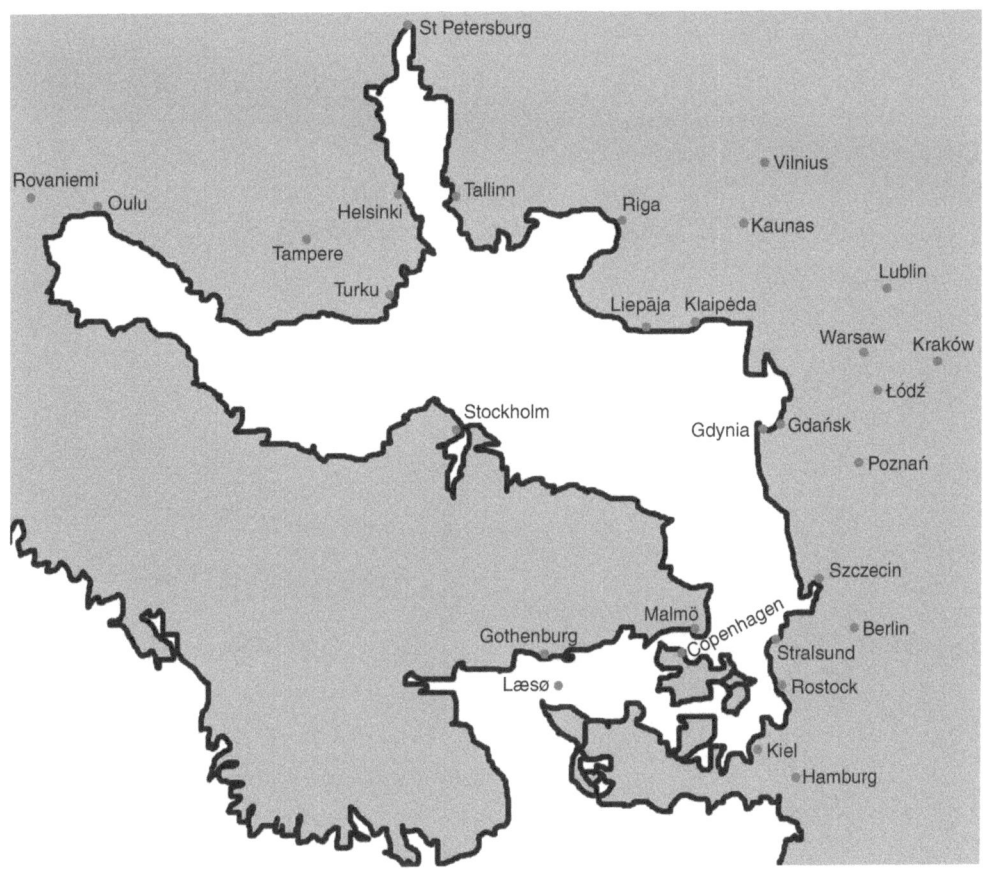

The Baltic Sea

The following stories were gathered between
25 January 2016 and 19 January 2017

1
Beginnings

'The worst grandmother in the world!'
Vita Khlopova, Moscow

I was dancing everywhere.

Once, when I was about six years old, I had a little fight with my grandmother in the street because she told me 'we need to go home to eat'.

I said to her, 'no, I hate you, I need to spend more time in the street, you are the worst grandmother in the world!'

I was so expressive that one lady who saw me said, 'you know, tomorrow there will be the last examination for the USSR Olympic reserve team for artistic gymnastics'.

She went on to say, 'only three girls from the USSR will be accepted'.

The next day I went to the exam with my grandmother. I did the exercises the jury told me to do, and that was it. We were packing up to go home and one of the jury members said to me, 'wait, why are you going?'

I said, 'there are over 300 girls here, of course I won't be accepted, I am just nobody'. Actually, it turned out that I was one of the three girls accepted.

My mother was shocked. I was living in a small town and it was 40 minutes' drive to Moscow, where the training was. It meant that my mother had to take me every day after school to this Olympic training.

She said to my grandmother and I, 'why did you do this?!', but I just loved it. This is the path that set me on the road to become a dancer.

The windmill
Marija Kaklauskaite, Vilnius

When I was little, like under the age of ten, there would be these commercials on television of a guy breakdancing. He was on the floor and spinning, doing a move called the windmill. I was really hypnotised by this movement, I just thought it looked so cool.

One day after seeing the commercial I went into my bedroom and tried out the move. There was carpet on the floor, but it didn't matter. I was just rolling all over the floor trying to do anything with my legs, it would have looked ridiculous, but it felt amazing.

I remember thinking 'oh my gosh, that is amazing, that feels so cool!'

Majia Rantanen, Espoo At first dancing was a total mystery to me, I couldn't see how to get my extremities to move at the right time in the right direction, and also coordinate all four limbs. It stirred whole new pathways in my brain. It was fun.

Love of my life
Maija Rantanen, Espoo

I watched the Eurovision Song Contest on television, and *Riverdance* was performed as the interval act. I remember thinking that it was so wonderful. After this I saw a dance school in Espoo advertising a *Riverdance* workshop. I decided to go. After the workshop I stayed on at the school and continued to take classes, but I had total ignorance about dance. I even asked the question, 'what is the difference between salsa and samba?', can you believe my total ignorance?

I am now 56 years old. I started to dance about 15 years ago, and it has grown to be the love of my life. It started from random weekly classes to the point where I now know different Cuban orishas, the difference between son and son montuno, and all the wonderful world of Cuban rumba. Sometimes I take five classes a week, different dances with different teachers.

The communist way
Elwira Piorun, Warsaw

When I was a child, Poland was a socialist communist country. At this time there were no commercials on the television between programmes, rather there would be ballet – so there would be things like the *La Sylphide* pas de deux, or an excerpt from *Swan Lake*. The communist way was to give the viewers a little piece of art between the television programmes. I saw so much ballet on TV this way that I wanted to start learning ballet. It was not my parents' idea that I would go to ballet school; it was mine.

Holding each other's hands
Anni Pilhjarta, Rovaniemi

There's this photograph of my sister and I dancing. In the photo we are both wearing some sort of veil that was made out of thin white fabric, which our mum had put over our heads. I remember being in the living room with my younger sister, she's two years younger than me, and in the photograph we are dancing while holding each other's hands. I think that's the earliest memory I have of dancing.

My sister and I were dancing quite a lot when we were younger, or just moving around the house. This is one of the reasons why our mother decided to take us to folk dance classes. But also my sister had seen folk dance performances on TV and she said to our mother, 'I want to dance like that'. Our mother then saw an advertisement for a folk dance crew and training, and she took us along.

Take the boat
Anamet Magven, Læsø

I grew up in the very north of Denmark, on the mainland where you take the boat to the islands. There was no dance really happening there, there was a lot of gymnastics, so that is what I did.

My hero
Atte Herd, Rovaniemi

I started dance when I was around three years old. My mum was a dance teacher in a very little city called Iisalmi. So ever since I was born, I was always with her at rehearsals.

My earliest memory of dance is from when I was just three or four years old. My brother and I would often play around during rehearsals my mother was taking on the weekends, and I would always admire the young guys that were dancing.

There was one particular guy, Tuomas, who I liked to watch; he went on later to become a professional dancer. Tuomas was my hero at that time. Every time he didn't master a movement on his first try, he would just quit and come over to play with my brother and I in the hallway. I recall he would get frustrated and say, 'no! I'll never learn it, I never will, I'll just go play'.

Tuomas was a really good dancer, and he was always the one performing the solos. After a while he got more responsible, and he started to learn how to rehearse properly. Tuomas was always babysitting us during that time, and that influenced my decision of becoming a dancer too, because I wanted to be like Tuomas.

Second place
Satoshi Kudo, Stockholm

My plan was not to be a dancer; my dream was to be an actor. I was really into action films – Bruce Lee and Jackie Chan – typical for any boy really.

I studied gymnastics and martial arts, and when I was 18 I got into an acting school in Tokyo. This school was based on stunt man skills. Some of the graduates of this school are quite well known in Hollywood – actors who are in movies like *The Last Samurai, Kill Bill*. I studied there for a couple of years, and I was quite good at acting, martial arts and gymnastics, but my dance skills were never good enough. At the end of season exams I was always second place in the class, because my dance skills were not good.

I started to go to extra classes after school for dance. I started with jazz dance, back then contemporary dance was not so popular in Japan. I studied ballet and jazz dance, and I started to go into the musical world. So my initial idea was just to practice my dance skills to do better in my exams for my acting school, but it ended up that I found dancing to be more interesting.

Slipped into dancing
Magdalena Jankowski, Otrebusy

I kind of slipped into dancing.

My mum is a former dancer and there was not always a babysitter to look after me, so she took me to rehearsals, but she never forced me to start dancing myself. When I was about 15 years old she said to me, 'now you have to decide, if you want to do dance professionally you have to work more, and if not focus on something different'. So I decided to fulfil my dream of dancing.

I changed dance schools and I started to work harder. I moved out of my parents place at that time, and it was quite hard in the beginning, being 15 and living alone so I could pursue my dance career.

A cafeteria
Vytis Jankauskas, Vilnius

The first time I saw breakdance was in a cafeteria where there was a TV playing music videos. In this one music video I saw there was breakdance, but I didn't know that was exactly breakdance at the time. After seeing this I went to that cafeteria every day with my friends and waited for that video to play.

Swedish troll
Simone Höckner, Malmö

My mother was a modern dancer in Germany, and she and my father renovated a really big brewery into a dance studio. I remember that the ceiling was very high and there were a lot of lights everywhere.

My mother taught my first classes, and I remember she always had improvisation classes with a lot of fantasy in them. I remember she was always talking about this character of a Swedish troll. One of the things I can remember was my mother saying, 'now you move like a troll'.

I was only three or four years old, but I was so fascinated and proud of my mother when I saw her with the other children.

Be curious
Mart Kangaro, Tallinn

I began dancing by accident, and I started with ballet, but very late.

My friend went to a dance school and took me along. I got into the training, and she didn't. It was the early '90s, and the whole Soviet Union had just collapsed. Estonia was part of the Soviet Union, and the dance school system was based on ballet education.

While I was studying at ballet school I independently started to be curious about other dance approaches. I took classes at different studios to broaden my perspectives.

The local newspaper
Gosia Mielech, Poznań

I went to ballet school in Poznań when I was nine years old. Prior to that I didn't have any formal dance experience. I went to the school out of the blue, I didn't know anything about ballet.

My father saw an advert in the local newspaper about an open day at the ballet school. I went to the open day with my mum and I saw these beautiful sylph-like girls dancing and I fell in love!

I thought, 'I am going to go for it!'

I have two brothers and a sister, they are all older than me, and out of concern they were trying to discourage me, but I'd already made up my mind. At the school there were dance classes every day and regular school classes too – physics, math and things like that. Basically, the students are at the school for a minimum of 10 or 11 hours a day, so it is not easy. But for some strange reason I thought it was something for me, it was my own decision, and no one pushed me at all. It was actually even a little bit of the opposite; people were trying to discourage me. For some peculiar reason I just felt like it was the right thing to do.

Just jump
Edmundus Zicka, Vilnius

My first dance lesson was in a huge hall, and there were a lot of people and two teachers. The teachers said, 'now you will jump, and only jump'. Everyone was jumping, and then the two teachers chose the boys and the girls to join the dance class based only on how they jumped! That is how it began, with jumping – just jump and you will be a dancer.

Forest kindergarten
Iwona Wojnicka, Warsaw

My life started in deep communism, I was born in the far East of Poland, a long way from Warsaw.

My grandparents raised me and there was no kindergarten where we lived, so most of my activities I did by myself, including my dancing. I made my own kindergarten really, and now I think about it, it is like what they would call in Germany a *waldkindergarten*. I did this on my own.

My day would start at 9a.m., and it did not matter what the weather was, but between 9a.m and 3p.m. I would be outside. I would make activities to do with whatever was around me; I would play, jump, run and dance. I did not know that it would have such a profound impact on my life.

Swan Lake arms
Laura Lohi, Malmö

When I was five my mother put me in a dance class. I don't remember why. I remember that in the second class that I took I cried and said that I never wanted to be there again.

The only other memory I had from this class was that we were running across the floor while doing *Swan Lake* arms, and I thought that it was the most ridiculous thing – I was thinking what is this?

'Popping or locking?'
Tony Antanas Ceponis, Vilnius

I thought that moving like a robot would be a nice idea.

A friend, who also started dancing the same year as me, said, 'okay, you want to learn to do the robot? There is a studio nearby, come with me'. I went to the studio and it was hard, I could not pick up anything, but I loved it. I did not know anything about dance.

When I came here they had two styles, locking and popping. I went to register and the receptionist asked me, 'where are you going, to the class with popping or locking?'

I had no idea, I just guessed and said, 'popping'.

I guessed right, because that was where I learnt to move like a robot. I was lucky.

Tony Antanas Ceponis, Vilnius My parents used to say to me 'you should try dancing, you have good characteristics for it, you are flexible, you feel the music well'. I kept saying 'no, I will never be a dancer!'

Nadia Comaneci
Özen Erdinc, Malmö

I was moving all the time.

I was climbing the pipes in our apartment when I was four, five, six years old. I would climb up and lie on the hat shelves.

When my dad came home from working at the factory, and when I was home from school, we would have these workout sessions together. We had this long hallway coming into the apartment, with a very long carpet. So we had this session, where we did somersaults; he did it and I did it after, and then we would roll back and repeat everything again.

That was fun because in my childhood I was a big fan of Nadia Comaneci, the Romanian gymnast. In the courtyard of the school during breaks, my friends would always ask me to show them the splits over and over again.

Communist years
Piotr Zalipski, Otrebusy

My first dance teacher was my neighbour. He came to the apartment where I lived with my parents and he said to my parents, 'I will gather all the children in the apartment building and we will start a dance group'.

It was in the communist years, so this sort of thing was quite normal.

I remember that in this dance group we danced the Polish national dances, things like the Krakowiak and another dance from the Lublin region called the Osa.

Nirvana and Michael Jackson
Moa Westerlund, Stockholm

As a kid living with my mother and my brother, we had a stereo in our living room and I would dance around to whatever was playing.

My brother listened to Nirvana and Michael Jackson – I was born in the '80s – so this type of music was big then. But then in contrast I listened to Stravinsky, Vivaldi's the Four Seasons and I liked Freddy Mercury too.

So I started to dance in the living room, and I would have only been about four years old. I invited our neighbours to come and watch me dance. I would make a stage out of pillows, I would change the whole living room arrangement, and I would perform with the music.

The carpet
Modjgan Hashemian, Berlin

My earliest dancing memory goes back to around 1978 in Tehran, when I was four or five, just before the Iranian Revolution.

That was a time where I used to lock myself into a room where there was a Persian carpet, and I used to dance through the patterns of the carpet.

This was my first dance experience.

I remember this as a very pleasant memory, it gave me a lot of energy and I could lose myself in these patterns of the carpet. I was dancing for hours through the patterns, following them, interpreting them. At the time I could feel there was tension around me in Tehran, and this room and on this carpet was a place where I could let go.

Never just sitting down
Susanne Frederiksen, Copenhagen

I discovered ballet on the television. I wanted to become a ballet dancer and I was imitating what I saw on the TV.

My mother said to me, 'you will be too big, you will be too tall for ballet'. Actually, I think she was right; I was probably too tall.

But I have always been a moving person. It was not just dancing in the beginning, I was interested in expression – so it was dancing, music, theatre – I was never just sitting down, it was the physicality, the stories and the communication that was really attractive to me, even though I didn't really know that at that time.

Little battles
Njara Rasolo, Helsinki

In the block of houses where I lived all the guys would dance together. At that time we did mainly hip hop and street dancing. So there would be little battles here and there, and at that time I was still very young and I was looking up to the older guys.

An old radio
Oxana Bellamy, Helsinki

When I was small I listened to a lot of classical music because my father had an old radio that was on all the time. Russia at that time was very friendly with

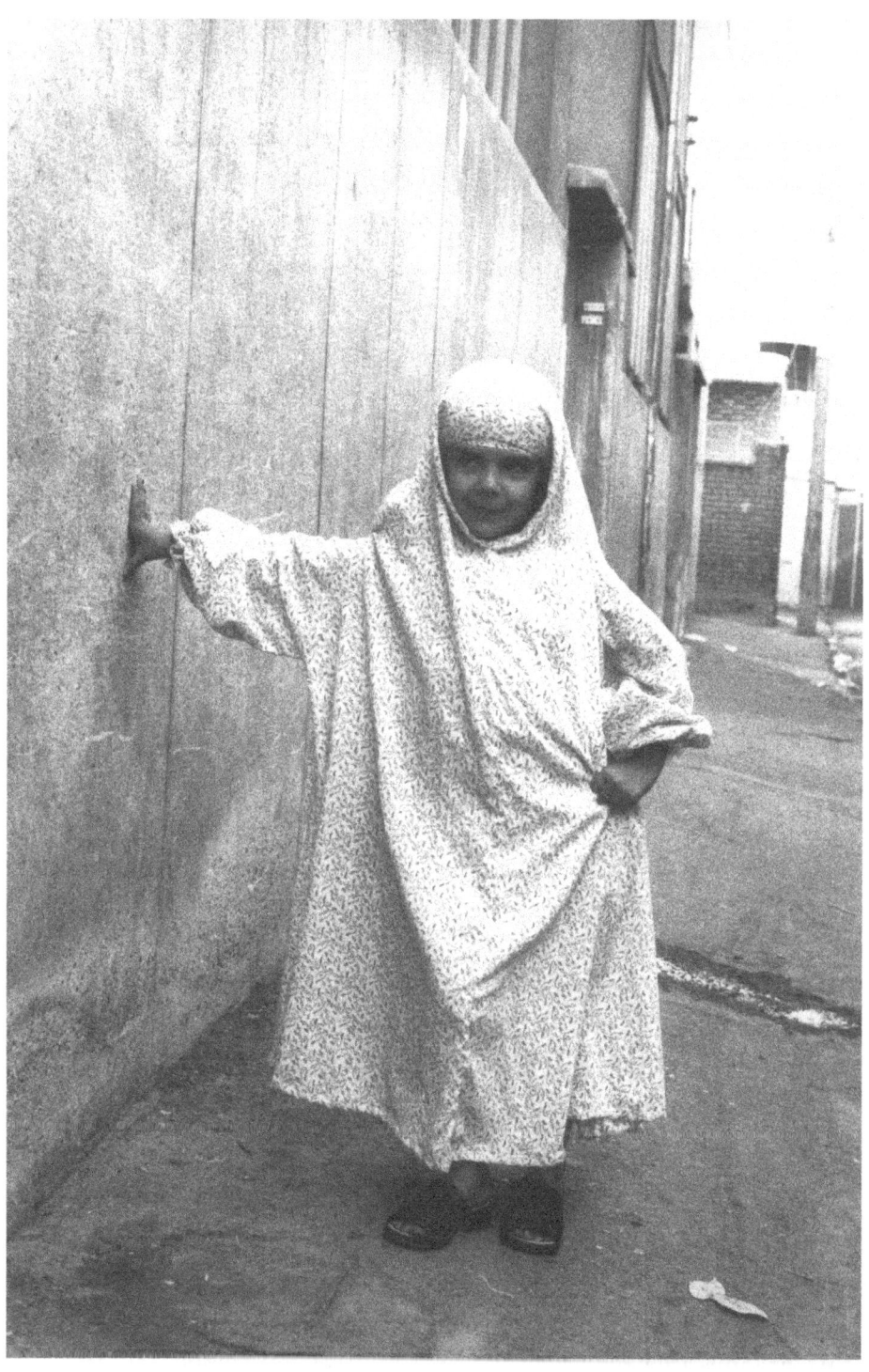

Modjgan Hashemian, Berlin When there was a party my family would say 'Modjgan, now it is your turn, come and dance!'

Rash Sensei, Copenhagen Dance is not only for happiness, to dance freestyle and have a good time. Dance is more than this and connects with real life.

Cuba, so the radio played a lot of Cuban salsa and Cuban songs, and I think these have stuck in my blood.

I recall standing in my very small baby bed, in my family's flat in the centre of St Petersburg, not far from Nevsky Prospect. I must have been just two or three years old. I remember that radio, the room and how small I was. But most of all I remember the music, the Latin music.

I think I only realised the significance of this early experience later when I came to Finland and I went to a Latina dancing school. There was something about that music that was with me.

Much cooler
Liva Zorgenfreija, Riga

I started with ballet, and the whole time I was doing ballet I would think 'folk dance? I don't think I really want to do that'. I was being a bit snobby about it, I was thinking that ballet was so much cooler.

After spending time abroad I came back to Riga and I wanted to dance. The folk dance festival was coming up, and I wanted to take part in this because I had seen it from the perspective of the audience and I thought it looked amazing.

Normally people are not accepted into folk dance groups so close to the festival, but because my mother had been a dancer in this folk group for a long time and my cousins had been too, my family was connected and because I had a good background in ballet I think they thought 'okay, we trust you'. So that is how I ended up being a folk dancer.

With my mother
Helmi Järvensivu, Rovaniemi

I was born into a family where dance is a daily affair. I started dancing in a dance school when I was two and a half years old.

But my earliest memory would have to be dancing with my mother in our living room. My mother and father were really interested in Finnish folk dance and folk traditions, so I think I was dancing some kind of children's song and dance in our living room.

Piotr Zalipski, Otrebusy The first time I saw Marowse Dance Group it was on TV; I was five or six years old. I remember that the finale of the dance looked like a big birthday cake. It was impressive and colourful, with a lot of people on the stage.

Dr Snuggles t-shirt
Özen Erdinc, Malmö

My fourth grade teacher, Sonia, noticed that I liked to move. I loved singing and I loved performing theatre, and just creating fun stuff in class. I was very active and very good at gymnastics, so she called my mum and told her that she saw an advertisement in the newspaper about an audition for the Malmö City Theatre Ballet School in spring.

My teacher thought that it was something that I should do. My mum was a preschool teacher and the audition was while she was working and she couldn't leave the kids. My mum said it was a nice idea, but she couldn't take me there. My teacher offered to take me there instead.

So one day, my teacher told me, 'remember to bring your gymnastics gear tomorrow, we are going somewhere after school'.

After lunch, she took me to the audition. She brought a bun of bread for me on the way, and walked to the audition with me. I was like, 'okay, what are we doing? Where are we going?' and I saw these girls in their pink leotards, and some of them even had tutus, and clearly they had done ballet or some dancing before. I was in red little running shorts, with a Dr Snuggles t-shirt on, just normal socks and had my hair in braids.

That was the year I turned 11.

The audition was over two days. The first day they were checking our bodies. We had to lie down and contract, extend our backs, stretch our feet and show our turn out. I remember that my toes were cramping. But of course, having this little competitive spirit, I was looking around and comparing myself to the others.

I remember when they were looking at our turn out, I was like, 'oh, what's that?' because everyone was in a frog position while I was struggling. I couldn't do it and I was questioning why. Then we had to move to music across the floor, just down up up, down up up, across the room.

After the first day, we were told who got through, and I was told to come back the next day. The next day, I went back and did the same thing.

The world opened up
Jo Parkes, Berlin

I read English and German literature at Oxford. There I had a professor who one day said to me, 'oh, you know who Pina Bausch is?'

I was like 'um, no…'.

He showed me *Café Muller* by Pina Bausch, and then the world opened up for me.

As soon as I saw this video I understood that some of the things that I could do came together. In the dance training that I had I felt that I had to switch off the intellectual side of myself, and after seeing *Café Muller* I thought, 'well I don't have to, this is completely what I want to do'.

A soldier
Krysztof Fijak, Otrebusy

I saw a folk ensemble on TV, and after that I said to myself, 'I have to dance'.

I found this ensemble near my home and began to dance. This was something odd, because no one in my family dances.

It was only when I was about 16 years old that I decided that I wanted to work as a professional dancer, but I did not have the required ballet training to do this immediately. When I graduated from middle school I passed the examination for the Dance Ensemble for the Polish Army in Warsaw. I was in the army for two years. I was a soldier at first, and after I completed my military training I joined the Dance Ensemble.

The doorway
Petezis Studens, Riga

My mother took me to a folk dance group for children when I was three years old, but the history of why she took me is more complex.

When my mother was young she went to ballet school, but to become a dancer was a dream for her that never came true. She was too short for the ballet company, and they were very strict on the heights of dancers. If you are too tall or too short you are just out of the game. However, the love for dance was then with her for all her life, and this prompted her to take me to dance school.

At first I was very shy, like *very* shy. I remember at one of my first classes I was standing in the doorway not going in. I just didn't want to move. I remember I said to the teacher, 'don't take me in there, I am afraid'. I don't remember what happened after that, but I must have gone in to the class eventually.

The band
Nina Hoikma, Rovaniemi

My father is a musician, and often when he would go on gigs, my family and I would go too.

In Finland, they are many restaurants where a band comes out at some point and people would pay for a ticket to dance – the band would play things like the waltz, polka, mazurka. Twice a year, my family and I would go to the north of Finland near Muonio, where there are a lot of skiing places – like Saariselkä and Olos. My father's band would be there for about a week playing in the restaurants, and my family would go along with the band, and the band's families, as well as some friends. People would go there on holiday to ski, and in the evening my father's band played, and we were there as well – listening and dancing.

I remember clearly dancing with my father's friend, who has since passed away. He was a tango senior, and he was a very good dancer. He was the one who taught me to dance slow waltz, the Viennese Waltz. I think I was about 12 years old then, I remember that I wasn't that tall dancing next to him. It felt like a very normal thing to do – just learning how to dance in this way.

A few seconds
Volker Eisenach, Berlin

I started dancing in 1986 in my Berlin school.

At school there was an afterschool dance group. It was different from regular classes at school, and you didn't get any grades – so getting grades wasn't the reason or motivation for me to go there. But this afterschool dance group had performances, often on a big stage with lots of lights, and an auditorium that would seat 400. I was fascinated by the stage, I loved circus and ice-skating shows and everything connected to performance.

I saw that they had this dance show coming up, and I thought, 'I want to be a part of that'. I had no clue what dancing meant. I said to myself, 'tomorrow, I am going there'.

I asked a friend of mine to come with me and he was like, 'no, I'm not going there'. It never came into my mind the question of 'is dancing done by boys or by girls?' I just wanted to do it. Then by coincidence I found out that four girls from my class wanted to go there for the first time that day too, so I thought, 'oh, that is great'.

So we went together. I remember before we entered the rehearsal space I had a brief moment where I thought, 'hmm, should I really go? Maybe it will be bad'.

I was so close to leaving, and then one of the girls said, 'let's go in there', so in I went. It was a decision I made in just a few seconds.

Daniel and Jessica
Anna Solakius, Lund

I started dancing salsa when I was 18 or 19 years old. I don't really know why, but I think I got really captivated by the music.

When I started salsa the problem was that there were too many women and not enough men dancing. I remember being really bored of waiting for a partner to become available, so I started to lead instead. A little while later one of the guys in my choir knew that I was doing salsa, so he asked if I wanted to try out tango with him. My first reaction was, 'oh tango! That sounds really boring'. I had this feeling that it was going to be very stiff and serious, whereas salsa to me was the opposite, just fun and loose. I was not very positive going in to that first tango class, but I still went.

I don't really remember much about the first class, but I do remember being completely mesmerised by the teaching couple – Daniel and Jessica. They were actually brother and sister, so that was quite funny or special, especially when you are dancing a tango. When they demonstrated a movement, I was completely blown away. I do remember Daniel's dancing in particular. I remember his facial expressions the most. I remember him looking sad when he was dancing, his eyebrows would go up a little and it looked like he was about to cry.

Feelings and emotions
Alyona, St Petersburg

I was not one of those people who had dreamed about dancing since I was a child, was not planning to do this. I did basic choreography at regular school, but since I was very young I have been interested in psychology. At university I decided to study to become a psychologist. But when I started to study this I realised that my interest in psychology was based on my own desire to go deeply into my own feelings and emotions.

I started to learn dance a little after this, and I went to lots of different dance classes. It was in these classes that I realised that dance could offer me what I was looking for in psychology – depth to explore and experience my feelings and emotions.

On the TV
Veera Lamberg, Helsinki

I have been dancing since I was three years old, and I have to say that I was pretty young when I knew that this was my 'thing'. I was really motivated and focused on dancing; my dream was to be a professional someday.

I remember many things from when I started dance, especially performances and the creative exercises that we did. I remember how I could really express my feelings. I went to the local dance school, near my home, but it was one of the biggest dance schools here in Helsinki. I was doing creative dance for children at the beginning, and then later this creative dance became contemporary dance. Then when I was about seven years old I started to do ballet classes.

It was my choice to dance, but my mother was also interested in dance because she danced when she was young. But my mum said that every time I saw something on the TV to do with dancing I would say, 'I want to do that!', so my mum took me to these classes, but she never forced me.

Two places in the car
Raivis Dzjamko, Riga

I actually started dancing quite late, in my teens. I started with Latvian traditional dance, and then there was a TV show that was looking for dancers. I thought, 'well, I can try out for it, I have nothing to lose'. I got accepted.

It was hard at the beginning.

I started on this TV show in winter and from my home to the TV studio I would have to catch one bus for one and a half hours, and then another bus for half an hour. Winter in Riga is cold, so I would get to the studio and would do aerobics to warm up. Over the winter months I would be the only dancer turning up, no one else would come because it was too cold.

I did the TV show for two years and each winter was the same. I was the only one who would be there on those cold days.

Because I went to every rehearsal I had a chance to do a special performance. The person who was coordinating the special performance was like, 'I only have two places in the car, who is coming?' Even though the other dancers were better than me and had more experience, she wanted to take me to this performance because I was always turning up.

Anna Paś, Otrebusy When I joined the ballet school my parents made it clear to me that going to such a school is not an additional evening class you can give up whenever you want, that it was something more serious.

Swinging on the barres
Ella Gröndahl, Oulu

I started dancing in Oulu, and the dance studio was in a basement-like room that was very dark. I would have been two or three years old. I remember that at this age I was not very good at leaving my parents, so I recall that before this I was kind of sad to go to the class. But I think I quickly forgot about it.

There were some ballet barres in the room, and I was hanging off them, swinging on them, like kids do. I remember talking with the other kids who were also swinging on the barres. I think we were talking about funny things like, 'do you know that horses leap? And they stand up when they sleep?'

After swinging on the barres for a while I remember the teacher saying, 'okay, get ready! Come here!' We stopped swinging and talking, and started dancing.

A lot of noise
Vita Khlopova, Moscow

My grandmother's work colleague said to her, 'my cousin is a Bolshoi dancer at the Bolshoi Theatre, she could have a look at your granddaughter and say if she is good or not'. My grandmother took me to Bolshoi to meet this dancer. It was my first time I was in the Bolshoi Theatre, and it was for *Swan Lake*. I remember how loud the pointe shoes were on the stage – for me it was not something magical, it was a lot of noise!

After the show this dancer, who was a soloist with the company, said, 'okay, show me what you can do'.

I think I did some splits or something and she said, 'okay, you are flexible, so your body is good for this. But never tell anyone in the Bolshoi School that you know me because the director hates me'.

This was my introduction to the ballet world!

I went to the Bolshoi Ballet School, and really, I didn't want to go there, it wasn't my dream; it was maybe the dream of my grandmother. But I easily passed the audition, so I started ballet.

Red tutu
Niina Vahtola, Oulu

The building I started dancing in was very old. It still exists in Rovaniemi where I live, and it looks in very bad condition from the outside. I definitely remember the rats in the building.

I really looked up and appreciated the older students at this dance school. I remember that there was this particular older dancer who caught my eye. I wanted to be like her. I thought she was amazing, and she is a person who has continued dancing ever since then.

When I was in the second grade, about eight years old, there was a drawing contest at our school. We had the task to draw: 'what do you want to be when you grow up?' Of course, I drew a dancer. I think I drew that dancer who had caught my attention. In my picture she had a very beautiful red tutu, and brown curly hair, and her leg was above her head. The painting was very colourful.

I thought that I would be like her, and I have told her lately that she was my inspiration.

An imprint on my mind
Vitaly Kim, St Petersburg

I was born in Uzbekistan. At that time it was quite a poor country. It was also a Muslim country, which meant that there was limited exposure to a diversity of culture.

But when I was in the tenth grade, so about 16 years old, I saw a performance of Butoh on the TV. I have no idea why it was shown on TV as the broadcasts were usually quite conservative, but I will forever remember what I saw. This performance was very inspiring, and watching it made me excited. It left an imprint on my mind, not just about the performance, but the idea that it was possible for the body to move in such a way has left a lasting impression.

2
Learning

'Are you going to spin on your heads?'
Mindaugas (Minda) Bruzas, Vilnius

When I started learning breakdance my friends and I just started to gather, and groups of us would train wherever we could. We would train in places like underground passages or sometimes in malls.

If the shopping malls had a free spot the security would let us train there, they would say, 'are you going to spin on your heads? Nice! Okay, go over there'. It was not like in the middle of the mall, more like corridors, corners, nooks, that sort of thing. Security would say, 'that's fine, just make sure you're not bothering anyone'.

Basically, all the places in Vilnius where they let us dance for free we have danced. When I look back on it now I realise how it was not a good place to train – the training time is always short, the floor is always hard and you get a lot of injuries.

'Good'
Anamet Magven, Læsø

My teacher always saw the dances I had made and said 'good'. She didn't do much to the dances, so I just kept on working. Sometimes she would just observe me while I was creating, so she would not really interfere.

I don't remember her really correcting me, I mean, maybe she gave feedback and if I had questions she would help me. I think she would have only done that if she thought what I was making was good enough.

Too young
Elwira Piorun, Warsaw

It was prestigious to be accepted into a ballet school, and I was accepted into the school in Poznań. Each year they accepted 20 students into the school. This was in 1969.

At the time, the ballet technique we learnt was the Vaganova style, and it was Russian pedagogy. There was really nothing else available here in Poland.

I had heard that there were other techniques, jazz, modern dance and things like that. But no one really knew what these dance forms were, and there were certainly no teachers or dancers who could share this knowledge. Because of the Iron Curtain we really only had access to what was happening in Russia.

There were some dancers who had travelled before World War II to train abroad and they had some knowledge, but I am a little bit too young and I missed out on that.

No windows
Anni Pilhjarta, Rovaniemi

My dance trainings were held in an elementary school. There was this shelter-like room, it was quite small with really thick doors, and it had no windows.

That's where we danced traditional Finnish folk dance, and some other dances that required singing while dancing. We were in a circle a lot, holding hands and galloping. I loved it!

Right from the beginning, I knew that that was what I wanted to do.

'Maybe some potatoes?'
Vita Khlopova, Moscow

I would work from 10a.m. until 3p.m. for the Moiseyev Dance Company. In the company I was the youngest artist, and the teachers and directors told me 'you should learn everything, you should do everything, this is your job'.

Then from 3p.m. until 7p.m. I went to the Moiseyev Dance School. Because I was a young artist from 7p.m. until 9p.m. I would have evening rehearsals.

I didn't even have time to eat, I would just drink something, maybe have some yoghurt, but nothing more, and the people in the company kept saying, 'you should never think you are better than we are because you are still in the school, and that is why you are dancing everything here'.

It was physically very difficult. I lost seven kilos, and I was only like 50 kilos to begin with!

When I went back home, my mother-in-law said to me 'are you hungry?'

I said, 'oh yes!'

She said, 'here is a little salad', I ate that.

She said, 'maybe soup?' I ate that in like three seconds.

Then she said, 'maybe some potatoes?'

I was like 'of course!'

And afterwards she would always give me some dessert.

Marija Kaklauskaite, Vilnius The first tricky thing I learnt was how to stand on my head and spin on it. It was really fun because not many girls around the world can do it, and here in Lithuania not that many boys can do it even, so it is a little bit special.

Little critic
Marija Kaklauskaite, Vilnius

When I first started dancing I was enjoying the possibility and opportunity of attending the hip hop battles. Later on after I discovered my capabilities and what I could do, there would always be that feeling of 'I could've done better'.

I think I will always have that little critic in me, reminding me I could've done more. But I figure that it's okay because that's how you learn – you mess up once and you want to try again until you get it right.

Jumping, jumping, jumping
Oxana Bellamy, Helsinki

My parents took me to ballet school when I was six years old. I remember that I passed to get in. I was there for half a year, and I remember that it was very hard training. We were jumping, jumping, jumping, higher, higher and higher.

Confused
Laura Lohi, Malmö

I don't remember being nervous when I auditioned for ballet school, because it wasn't like I had the dream of becoming a dancer. Even after ten years of dance education, it was never my passion, though I enjoyed it a lot. I guess at that ballet school audition I was a little confused, as I didn't really understand what was happening, or what it would lead to.

I knew that somebody there told me that I have some talent, and have the ability to do well, and said things like 'if you stretch more, you can do the splits in two weeks'. But I didn't want anything; I just went there and did what they told me to do.

Tools that I have
Gosia Mielech, Poznań

Everything changed when Ohad Naharin and his assistant Yoshifumi Inao came over to the Polish Dance Theatre. They changed my life as a performer, dancer, artist and as a human being.

When I discovered Gaga I changed my perception on movement. Gaga, for me, is not only a language of movement, but in a way it is a lifestyle. Since my first encounter with Gaga I have done intensives in this practice in many different places: Oslo, Barcelona, Berlin and Tel Aviv. It transformed me, my movement changed drastically, I became so much more aware and I wouldn't follow a pattern any more.

I was finally getting to know the tools that I have in my body.

I cannot stand words
Maija Rantanen, Espoo

For me personally, dancing has a healing power.

As a translator, my head is full of words. Sometimes after hectic working periods I feel I cannot stand words anymore. I would not want to read or even listen to radio in my free time.

The physicality of dancing, the rhythms, basic drums and melodies stir other parts of my brain, and after dancing I can stand words again.

Maija Rantanen, Espoo Soon one class a week was not enough. I found myself dancing three, even four times a week.

Njara Rasolo, Helsinki I started learning dance on the concrete streets in Madagascar, I still have scars on my back from this.

A school boy
Edmundus Zicka, Vilnius

When I was in the tenth grade my dancing teacher said that I could dance in Sietuva Dance Company, a folk dance group here in Lithuania. So I, as a school boy, went to the university student company. It is not a big company, but my dance technique grew rapidly by working with these older dancers. After a few weeks I went back to my regular dance classes at school and everyone saw that I'd improved.

Snow White has black hair
Modjgan Hashemian, Berlin

My mother put me through very traditional classical ballet classes and I did it for a long time until I got fed up because I was always playing the same roles. I was always Snow White, because Snow White has black hair, and I was the only girl in my class with black hair, I was so fed up with it because I also wanted to dance as the snowflakes because I thought that would be more fun.

I remember also standing at the barre one day, doing the ballet exercises. I was looking out the window and out into the street and I realised that 'wow, there is life out there, and what is happening out there interests me more than the pure technique I am learning in this studio'.

So there I was, when I was quite small, feeling there was something rebellious inside of me.

One in a million
Anni Pilhjarta, Rovaniemi

When I was eight years old I read a book about dance, and I remember that the main character in the book was named Trina. In the book it says something like, 'only one in a million can be a really good ballerina'. That sort of got my attention, and I decided that I wanted to be a ballerina.

I wasn't trained in ballet at that point, so I started writing down all the ballet terms in French in an old book, and that's what got my mother to start thinking about sending me to ballet classes, which she eventually did. I was nine years old when I started doing ballet.

On the beach
Magdalena Jankowski, Otrebusy

I started to take some lessons in Polish folk dance. The classes were for Polish expats living in Germany, and they happen in summer for three weeks. Over the three weeks specific dances and songs from different regions of Poland are taught.

I have to admit that my mum convinced me to do it.

At the beginning I thought, 'oh my God, only old people would be interested in this'. I thought it was ancient and that nobody would really care about it. So when my mother tried to convince me I was like 'no I'm not going, it will be boring and I want to spend my summer on the beach!' She then told me it was for young people. She played some of the music to me, and she showed me some of the material. I was more interested after this and I said, 'okay, okay I will try it'.

Dance party
Vytis Jankauskas, Vilnius

I learnt dance with my friends, we taught each other, we copied videos and we made things up. At first we just danced in the streets and then we tried to do it at a school.

At the school dance party we showed our first dance, and then had to write an explanation to the administration of the school for inappropriate behaviour.

Vytis Jankauskas, Vilnius I tried to get into every workshop possible, it was still quite difficult to travel abroad, but quite a lot of people came to Lithuania, so I took all the workshops I could.

Vytis Jankauskas, Vilnius The government at the time saw the dancing I was doing as a bad influence from the West; they saw it as a political thing, to the point where the KGB would get involved.

A puzzle
Vita Khlopova, Moscow

When I was studying in Russia and learning dance history it always ended with the work of Sergei Diaghilev. There would be a few lessons on Soviet ballet history, mainly about Yury Grigorovich, and that was about it. There was no Martha Graham, no Merce Cunningham, no Preljocaj, nobody. The whole twentieth century was eliminated.

When I went to France, everyone already knew this history, and I was like 'Cunningham? What? Who?'

In my Master's courses at the Sorbonne there were seminars about the aesthetic philosophy of Cunningham, and for me it was difficult. I didn't even know who he was! It was like a puzzle, I would just get Cunningham and then like two months later I would figure out that he was connected to Martha Graham. And on it went. In the three years I was studying in Paris I didn't see much of the city because I was so busy studying, and I was spending the whole time in the Centre National de la Danse.

After three years of studying in France, I learnt some things that I had *never* even heard about in Russia. I returned to Moscow with all this knowledge. I was like, 'I need to tell someone about all of this!'

I went to the Bolshoi Ballet School thinking they might want to include this in their dance history course, and they told me, 'we are not interested'.

I asked, 'why not?'

They said, 'because our students have to dance only *Swan Lake* or *Sleeping Beauty*, and they don't need to know more'.

I was like 'that is not true, your students go abroad'.

They said, 'that is not our problem, they can go abroad, but the aim is that they just go to the Bolshoi, and in the Bolshoi we don't dance Cunningham'.

Names of the exercises
Piotr Zalipski, Otrebusy

After working all day dancing I would spend one hour more on ballet. It was hard to remember and learn the names of the exercises. It is easy now, now I know.

Tony Antanas Ceponis, Vilnius If you don't have clean technique it is hard to make your dancing beautiful. So to get this technique it is torture!

Two pirouettes and a finger snap
Susanne Frederiksen, Copenhagen

I had a jazz ballet teacher called Doug Crutchfield. I had heard about him and I saw something in the papers about his classes, so I said to my friends, 'let's go there!' My two friends and I went. My friends quit after some time, but I stayed.

In jazz ballet I was not the sort of person who was doing two pirouettes and a finger snap, it was not really me. I was looking for something else.

After about a year of jazz ballet Doug said to me, 'I will have a teacher coming from the Martha Graham School, I think you should try this sort of dance'. So I tried it, and I was like, 'this is what I want to do!' I was like 'ta-da! I want to have a dance education, and I want to become a dancer!'

Nureyev jumping around
Volker Eisenach, Berlin

I thought about how when I was working with Royston Muldoom he told me that I should become a dancer. I really couldn't stop thinking about his suggestion. I thought, 'I love this dancing so much, is there really a chance for me to become a dancer, and what does that mean?'

I was still doing work with Royston, and was building up courage to talk to him about it. One day I lurked in front of his hotel waiting for him to come out, and then asked him these questions like 'so, if I want to become a dancer what do I need to do? What does it mean?'

He said, 'well, the first thing that you need to do is classical ballet'.

I was like 'what? Wait a minute, I want to become a dancer, I don't want anything to do with classical ballet, and tights and tutus'.

He was like, 'no, even if you want to become a contemporary dancer you still need a classical ballet foundation'.

He gave me names and addresses of two schools. I checked them out and went and did an audition, even though the school year had already started.

I had no knowledge of ballet, and for one of the schools I was just not good enough, I was so bad and I did not feel at home there with all the girls wearing buns in their hair. At this school I had a health check and they said to me, 'stand in second position'.

I was like 'umm, what is second position?'

Then they were like, 'no, I don't think this is going to work'.

I was like 'yeah, I don't want to be here anyway'.

The other school Royston mentioned was the Rambert School in London. Before the audition for Rambert I thought, 'okay if I have to do ballet I should probably go and do a ballet class at least once, then I can tell him I have done it'.

I went to the ballet class, and the guy at the front desk said that class would be with this lovely lady from the German Opera, and I was like 'the German Opera... okay'. I walk into the studio and see the teacher. She a tiny 45-kilo blonde lady, like really thin, a typical ballet dancer. We did the first exercise and she said, 'oh, there is a new guy, hello'. I was there in my tracksuit pants, and I was trying to stretch all my movements really strong. We did one or two exercises, and she made a joke and said to me, 'come on, what are you doing, is this like your first ballet class?'

I said, 'yes'.

She looked shocked and replied, 'really?'

I said, 'yes, really'.

She said, 'actually, you're doing really well'. We did two or three more exercises and then she said, 'are you sure this is really your first ballet class?'

I said, 'yes, it really is'.

I mean it was not like I was Billy Elliot or Rudolf Nureyev jumping around the room, but I knew how to move and I could follow the exercises. I did not know the technical terms, and I didn't have brilliant feet – I still don't – but I wanted to move, and I really wanted to work, and I think she could see that. I really enjoyed the class. I said that I would come back, and I did.

Zero points
Maija Rantanen, Espoo

I'll never forget the first time I got my steps correct in the choreography. Each step had a place and there were no extra steps. Each step had a meaning, and I got it right. For style I perhaps got zero points, but the idea of dancing was dawning on me.

Without any agenda
Mart Kangaro, Tallinn

My dance education happened in a certain time in Europe where there were so many new things happening. All of a sudden everything was free, you could travel, choreographers from Europe and from the United States and from all over the world came to Estonia.

I took all the workshops I could, without any agenda, I was just curious.

The whole system in the country was changing from being very limited in information, and having just one dance aesthetic that has dominated for a long period of time, to all of a sudden there is everything. I finally got to understand what was interesting for me, and it was long after dance school.

Ballerina style
Liva Zorgenfreija, Riga

There are specific steps for Latvian folk dance. At the beginning I was not very good, I also had a bit of a ballerina style, which is not good because it is a dance group. You have to behave as a group and perform as a group, and if you are standing out it is not a good thing at all! In ballet if you are a bit better or your leg is higher it is seen to be good, but here if your leg is higher its like, 'come on, what are you doing? Don't do that!', so that was a little hard to get used to.

No right or wrong
Modjgan Hashemian, Berlin

I applied to a school to study choreography, and I got accepted. I was a little bit surprised and thought to myself, 'wow', because it was a really famous school. I was thrilled that I could do this.

But then I started studying at the school, and I was so upset because I realised that in this institution there were a lot of professors who are from a 'classical direction' of making choreography. I don't want to say that a classical direction in choreography is bad, or wrong or anything, but it is a certain type of education and the hierarchy is very strong and clear, and I think this was not a pleasant learning experience for me.

I feel that I can learn more when I am comfortable, and people can see eye to eye. I certainly learnt some things when studying at this school, but in my opinion, they should not teach you *how* to then put it all together, and this *how* was getting too much. I much prefer that I take the tools, and the how to make a dance someone else can keep, I will find my own *how*.

Pictures to prove it
Vita Khlopova, Moscow

I was at the Bolshoi Ballet School for six years. I did one year of preparation and then five years of formal school education. The whole course is eight years long.

The problem was that I was small, and now there is the trend for tall ballerinas. My teachers told me 'you're good at folk dance, so maybe try that, because you will never be able to dance in the corps de ballet because you are short, so you'd have to be the best soloist'. Of course I would never become a soloist, I was good – I have some pictures to prove it – but I wasn't the best one. So that is why I switched to folk dance. I really didn't want to do this, but I didn't feel I had a choice.

Here in Russia we have a very famous dance company called the Moiseyev Dance Company. They are really famous; in the Soviet times even Bolshoi Theatre didn't have permission to go abroad, only Moiseyev Dance Company did. They dance folk dance from all over the world, and it is so technical. I did an audition with them, and I was dancing some Spanish dance with splits and things. They could see I was flexible and I think they thought, 'okay, wow, a ballerina in our folk dance company'.

Money and time
Oxana Bellamy, Helsinki

I really got into dancing when I was working, and I finally had money and time. I went to Zumba, and this woke me up. I thought, 'this, I really like!' I thought I could move a bit better than other people and I was looking for another type of dance, something Latino. Then I started to go to my salsa school, which is a Cuban dancing school.

Now I have started, I cannot stop. It has been five years. Basically I am hooked.

Not stylish
Petezis Studens, Riga

As a boy I learnt dance, but a bit later, in my teenage years I started to struggle. Each Autumn, when the dancing would start again I would tell my mother, 'this is the last year, after this I will quit, I am done'. I think the whole group of guys I was dancing with was thinking this, because it was not stylish for the guys to be dancing.

At the same time I started to play basketball, and it was like two totally different worlds, and none of my mates from basketball danced. But there was something in the dancing that kept me going back.

'We need you'
Volker Eisenach, Berlin

I came back from doing a performance in Duisburg and I had two letters in my letterbox. One said, 'you have an audition at Rambert Dance School, please come, it is in one week's time'. The second letter was from the German Army, and said, 'we need you'.

I went to Rambert, did the audition there and I passed. The audition was a real cliché, I had the t-shirt on with the number pinned on the front, and I was number five. A few weeks later I got a letter from Rambert saying, 'congratulations, we want you, please come'. But there was this problem because I still had the letter from the German army saying, 'we need you'.

Before the unification of Germany all men living in West Berlin did not have to go to the army, but since unification in 1990 there were no new laws existing about this – everyone was confused, did the men from West Berlin really have to join the army now? Nobody knew, and there was no one to ask, because nobody knew.

When the army sends the first letter saying, 'we need you' you're not allowed to leave Germany for longer than three months without permission for about two years. I had to stay in Berlin and go to university. I was studying to become a primary school teacher. I was not enjoying it.

Three years later I was still at the university, and suddenly I got a letter from the German army that said, 'we will never, ever, ever take you'. I was like, 'thank you, three years later!'

At 5a.m.
Vita Khlopova, Moscow

I was living in this little city far from Moscow. I had to wake up at five o'clock to get to the Bolshoi Ballet School at eight o'clock. From 9a.m. until 6p.m. we had dance classes and school subjects, and then it would take me two hours to get home. Then I would have to do one hour of gymnastics, one hour of homework and one hour of music and at 1a.m. I would go to sleep, to wake up at 5a.m. again.

It was really hard. So that is why my parents decided that I should live at the Bolshoi School, in the boarding school. In Russian it is so funny because the word for boarding school, **школа-интернат**, translates a little bit like an 'orphanage' in English. When I told all my friends that I am going to live at the Ballet School there they were all like, 'oh, we are so sad to hear that', and I was like 'no, no, no, it is not like that!'

Getting the stars
Cher Geurtze, Copenhagen

When I was seven years old I was sent to the local dance school, it was with a tap teacher and every time you learnt a step she gave you a star. The stars were the motivation.

Early on I disliked the whole system. There was something about it that was not at all creative, it was just based on coming in, learning the steps as quickly as possible, getting the stars, comparing yourself with the person next to you about how many stars you had, and it just seemed totally worthless.

Freeze
Raivis Dzjamko, Riga

There was something about the stage that made me feel alive, it gave me a sense of freedom. I just knew I wanted to be there, I wanted other people to look at me, which is really strange because I was always shy, really shy.

As a kid I was fine if I was dancing around on my own, but as soon as people came into the room or looked at me I would freeze, and look at the floor.

Winter conditions
Oxana Bellamy, Helsinki

In the Nordic countries when it is dark and cold for a good part of the year you need something to shake you, wake you up and escape. Otherwise in these winter conditions people start to eat a lot, some people drink a lot, they put weight on or they get depressed. In such conditions you need a change and something to look forward to.

When I started dance classes I was overweight, because in Finland if you have nothing to do you just eat and eat. But then I started dancing and I easily lost weight, I can feel confident and that I can control my body and my muscles. I feel stamina inside and that I am blooming.

Dark wooden floors
Anna Solakius, Lund

When I was three years old I was dancing around in a little pink leotard and a little skirt. It was at children's dance and I remember I had this really nice teacher.

There were a lot of kids in the class. The room was typically Scandinavian, with dark wooden floors, like a Tarkett, but quite shiny. I just remember this feeling, of you know you have these kinds of socks, with plastic on the soles, so you could run and you wouldn't slip.

Like drugs
Vitaly Kim, St Petersburg

I was searching for a place where I could find the sort of Butoh movement I'd seen on TV, or maybe something even close to this in the city where I lived.

I started to take part in activities at a theatre, it was Grotesque theatre, but based on the Stanislavski system. It was just a little group of us, and we worked

Vitaly Kim, St Petersburg I think that the group I work with are starting something that is foundational for dance films here in Russia. We might not end up being famous, but we are starting things here for the next generation.

really hard to develop theatre and dance, we all wanted to go deeper with movement and the roles we were exploring. At this time thought I was only working with dance movement as part of the theatre work.

I remember in the year 2000 the group of people I was working with and I started to push the lines of theatre a little more, in the plays we had been doing there was the text and we had the role, but between this there were pauses, and we started to realise that this pause was an important part of what we were doing. After this we tried to explore this idea and question 'if we do a play based only on pauses, what would that be like?'

We worked with this idea for a few months, and that is how we started to work with more experimental ideas, starting to think about what happens after the pause, after stopping all visual movements, what is happening in the body when you are doing nothing?

We were very young at this time, we were very free, and we worked seven days and all weekends – day and night. I realised that this kind of work was like drugs, I wanted more.

A language
Raivis Dzjamko, Riga

To begin with I was not so nervous about dancing on stage, it was only once I started to learn about technique that I started to get nervous. Sometimes the more you get to know about something the more nervous you get! It took me a few years to become more relaxed with this, and not worry so much about the technique.

I think learning dance technique is like learning a language, I remember that to begin with when I was trying to learn English I tried to force it and I was so worried about it. Then one day something clicked and I was like, 'wow, I know what they are saying, I understand, and I am replying easily'. The same with French, just one day it started to work and then I worried less about it. I think it is the same as learning dance technique, at first it is a big worry, and then over time it gets easier.

80 pages
Vita Khlopova, Moscow

For my final study at university, I decided to research the French choreographer Angelin Preljocaj. I went to the library in Moscow to see if there was anything on him at all, and there was nothing, not one thing in Russian. I thought, 'okay, in two months I have to hand in 80 pages of writing and I have nothing to go off'. This was in 2005, and there was not so much stuff on the internet.

I told my husband that I was struggling to find information, and he said to me, 'just write to Preljocaj'.

I said, 'he will never answer!'

My husband was like, 'just do this'.

So I wrote to him and then 20 minutes after sending the email I got a reply saying, 'okay, 7 April Preljocaj will be waiting for you in France if you'd like to meet'.

I was like 'okay…'.

My husband and I went to Paris so I could do the interview with Preljocaj. The interview went well and Preljocaj gave me a lot of material, more than enough for my university work.

While we were in Paris my husband said, 'there is the Sorbonne here, maybe there is some dance and theatre studies there for you?'

You can imagine, I was like 'I am a dancer, I don't speak French, and it is the Sorbonne!'

My husband insisted that I go and take my documents to the Sorbonne, so I did and they said, 'you're accepted, you just have to pass your French exam'.

So I had the whole summer of six hours per day of French studies preparing for this exam. For me, going to do this French exam was no big deal, I thought 'oh I'll just like be going to France for one week, do some exams and maybe one day I can tell my friends that I nearly got into the Sorbonne, and my level was quite good but not good enough to get in'.

But I passed the exam. I thought it would be so stupid if I did not take this opportunity. My husband said, 'of course you should go there'. I spent three years there studying.

My ponytail
Simone Höckner, Malmö

I had never done jazz before, because in Malmö, we didn't have jazz classes. When I arrived at my first class I noticed that everyone else had jazz pants on, while I had ballet clothes and tights on.

The teacher was a really big man, and he always had the same coloured shoes and clothes, matching colours and he wore big golden rings. He instructed us to move across the floor, doing pas de bourrée and other moves. I was just confused looking at him; I knew nothing about jazz.

When I am nervous, I start laughing – so I was laughing the whole way as I went across the floor in the studio doing the exercise he set. I saw him becoming more and more irritated as I travelled across the floor. At the end of the exercise he took me by my ponytail, and took me out of the class, and told me to stay there. I was in shock; it was terrible. After that every time in class, he would always look away from me, so I thought that he really didn't like me at all.

Three years later, I met the teacher again. He looked at me and said, 'hello Simone, that ballet girl'. I was never the ballet girl.

One-two-three
Magdalena Jankowski, Otrebusy

I was learning a dance from the south of Poland, from the Tatra mountain region.

It was really difficult to learn the steps for this dance, and it is one of the only Polish dances that is not a couple's dance – in this dance the men dance separately and the women dance separately.

I remember that everyone in the dance group was learning everything, all the girls were learning the male steps, and the men were learning the female steps, so we could teach the whole dance if we have students in the future.

The male steps are really difficult and the counting of the rhythm is different to what the music is telling you. For example, you have the counts in the music of 'two-one-two-one-two', but you're dancing 'one-two-three, one-two-three'. It's really confusing!

Not really in my blood
Susanne Frederiksen, Copenhagen

My dance teacher told me that there was this place called the London Contemporary Dance School, and maybe I should go. I went for an audition and I didn't get in because my ballet was not good enough. I came back home to Denmark and I started to train in ballet.

I felt like this was difficult because ballet was not really in my blood, even though I have a lot of turn out and my feet are the right way for ballet. I wanted to do something else, something more down to earth.

3
Making

Eating a pizza
Volker Eisenach, Berlin

In 1992, before I was supposed to leave for London, some friends and I were sitting around eating a pizza and they said, 'let's do a performance, a farewell performance before you go to London'.

I was like 'yeah, that sounds fun'.

So we thought that I could do the choreography, my friend was a composer and he could do the music, and two girls there were like 'we can write the story'.

The next day we talked about it again and thought it was still a good idea.

We asked all our friends, 'do you want to be in it?'

We then did the performance 80 days later and it was a huge success.

During the rehearsals for this 'farewell' performance I found out I couldn't go to London at that time. So it was not a farewell performance at all in the end.

One day before the performance we were all sitting around saying, 'okay, we need to know at least what the title of the performance is and we have to have a group name'.

One guy said, 'let's call it 'Faster-Than-Light''.

I said 'yeah that sounds good, but let's add 'Dance Company' at the end'.

Faster-Than-Light Dance Company still exists 24 years later, which is funny, since at the beginning it was just one 'final' performance.

Volker Eisenach, Berlin For all Light Dance Company projects the participants never have to pay, they are always free and we take everybody. There are never auditions and we always try not to make it like pop idol or dance idol where there is one person at the centre of the show.

Around the swings
Anamet Magven, Læsø

I was able to do my own choreography and I showed it from a young age. I would choreograph in the garden with a couple of girl friends, and we would put on a mixed tape and perform our routines to this. Of course it was in the field of gymnastics, so all about tricks, and it was about combining these tricks and then putting some costumes on – but of course there was that sense of creating something yourself.

I have this early memory of playing in the garden around the swings, and we would just put the radio on and take turns dancing and the other ones watching. So it was around this swing structure, inventing the movement with whatever was on the radio.

World of TV
Edmundus Zicka, Vilnius

I'm working on a dance TV show where dancers are dancing with famous singers from Lithuania. Each singer has a dance group for the TV show and each week the singers compete. So now I am living in this world of TV.

Because it is for TV, TV does not want the traditional folk dance staging. They want rock music, maybe retro music, maybe jazz music, the singers want to sing new songs, not old songs. So we have to get creative, we have to make some new things, it is very interesting for me. I mean maybe the dance we make for the TV show isn't even folk dancing.

The first dance that we are doing is retro style, so not folk dance, it's Eastern European retro style!

Snowballing events of activation
Alexa Wilson, Berlin

The work that I make often gets called 'complex' and 'bold'.

Questioning is one thing that comes up for me in my work and there is always ambiguity, there are never quite answers to questions. Then there is activation, and in some ways they kind of go together, because activation creates questions and questions can activate. But the activations come through in a much more bold, clear political imagery or statements, or provocations or evocations. These statements, as much as they might seem like they are pointed in one direction, are actually open, because as we see in the world today there are these snowballing events of activation that are happening worldwide, they don't just have one response.

A pirate themed dance
Atte Herd, Rovaniemi

My first choreography was when I was about 13 years old.

I was teaching an all boys class where we did basic acrobatic movements, such as cartwheels, and that was when I got this idea of doing a short dance. I had the idea to do a pirate themed dance for all the boys in the class. I cast my younger sister to play a witch, and the pirate boys chased her around and defeated her at the end of the dance.

That is my very first memory of choreography.

What do you want to tell?
Satoshi Kudo, Stockholm

I was sitting with Ana Laguna, Mats Ek's wife, who is a good friend, and I asked her if she could come and see the solo I had been working on. While we were in the studio Mats came in, and he was like, 'oh really, you want to make a piece? That's great'.

He asked one question, 'what do you want to tell?'

Not 'what do you want to *do*?' But 'what do you want to *tell*?'

I was so nervous, but this was so direct, and I thought, 'well, what do I want to tell?' I hadn't ever thought about it.

I don't think I will ever forget this. I think it is so often that we are asked, what do you want to do, or what is the idea? But we are not asked so often, what do you want to tell? Or what do you want to say?

Rash Sensei, Copenhagen I came here, to Denmark, two years ago, to seek asylum. My crew and I were talking about politics in our dances, and in the Congo we had a lot of problems because of this.

So it was a great question. I don't know if I answered it well for him in the moment, but it was a great gift from him, it was a lesson.

A 'fish tank'
Gosia Mielech, Poznań

Creating *Anonymous* was an amazing experience. It was a solo dance but I worked with two girls on aspects of it – Olga, who was a visual artist from Warsaw, and Ania, who was a composer and DJ from Wrocław. We had a meeting point in Poznań. Ania and Olga had never really worked with dance before. I really love to work with people who don't know dance because their minds are so open.

The performance *Anonymous* has live mapping and unique electronic music. I had the chance to perform it all over Europe. That was like a turning point for me as an individual, because I would never in my wildest dreams think that I would create a solo. You need to be very confident as a performer, you are totally exposed, there's nothing or no one to hide behind.

Gosia Mielech, Poznań The satisfaction of creating something – being able to express your thoughts and abstract thinking through movement to take the audience on a journey – it's so powerful, and it is addictive as well.

It is interesting because when I was creating this solo, part of the creative process took place in a container. The container had windows on each side, but it is like a small box, maybe five by three metres. It was placed in the centre of Poznań, on the edge of a very busy street. This container is usually used as an art gallery for a wonderful photographer who does black and white photographs. The photographer and I had a meeting, and he said, 'you can have the space to do whatever you want', so I decided to devote the time to experiment and work on creating choreographic material for the *Anonymous* piece.

I started to develop the work inside this container that was like a fish tank, completely exposed to the public: people passing by, cyclists and drivers. I felt both vulnerable and empowered. I had to fight with my ego, to avoid letting my ambition win and dancing my heart out, instead of staying true to my work and trying to build something substantial and develop certain ideas in that little container.

Curse and yell
Niina Vahtola, Oulu

There was this choreographer I worked with who was totally insane, but very interesting. She was doing very interesting choreographies in folkdance.

She would curse and yell at the dancers. She told me that the reason why she cursed and yelled at us was because she wanted us to find the real emotion in our dancing. And she did, when she was yelling we became much more emotional.

She also saw something in me. We did a performance where I was a main character, and it was very strange because I was a flute player in the group, not a dancer and I just hopped in to the dancing and she made me the main character.

On an outside stage
Elwira Piorun, Warsaw

The time came when I was too old to be a soloist in the ballet company, so I started to choreograph. Then I had the idea to make an evening of young choreographer's work. So I arranged this, and I danced in it too.

Thinking about it now, it was kind of in the style of Jiri Kylián. The piece that I made was on an outside stage, and it was with my friends from the ballet, who were the dancers in it. In this piece I was looking for new movement, to leave classical movement in some way. It was very difficult for me to find my style.

Movement is just movement
Atte Herd, Rovaniemi

I mainly approach choreography with a contemporary movement language, but I don't restrict myself in one particular style. I just borrow whatever I need from the different genres. There can be speech, there can be folk dancing, and there can be breaking dancing. I think that movement is just movement, I do dance, I don't just do contemporary dance.

I usually have a concept in my mind of what I would like to make, but I really don't know how it will play out. So I then go into the studio with my dancers, and we start making sketches, outlines for scenes to play out and how it will translate to the next scene, and it starts to take form from there.

Jump on the internet
Alexa Wilson, Berlin

I felt like my choreographic work had this political tone to it very early on, and it got labelled as anarchist and radical, words that are political labels.

Even though it was never like, 'I am a feminist, and I make feminist work', it was always implicitly coming through. I was questioning power structures basically, and I feel like Foucault is like been such a foundation for my whole career, and the foundation for questioning power structure. And being a woman that comes through as being feminist, which I am totally happy with.

I am exploring environmental politics, or socio-political dynamics, power dynamics in the work I make. When I worked with Touch Compass I was looking to explore the politics of privilege, now the questions have shifted more towards cultural questions of the other, who is Other-ed, outsiders and what are the dominant cultural voices versus the margins, and who is marginalised. Often it comes back to the same groups – women, non-white, indigenous, queer, disabled.

I feel like we are in a time when we need to ask these questions in a big way within society. You just need to jump on the internet and read these raging debates about racism in the USA, or indigenous issues in New Zealand, or the intense discussion about rape culture that is happening worldwide now. These debates are so lively right now, and it is validating to be a part of these larger conversations, but in a creative, abstract, performance context.

Old men
Iwona Wojnicka, Warsaw

I feel like now I am in an interval between two acts. That what has been has been the 'old' and we are waiting for the 'new' to start in relation to who will make choreographic work.

In Poland I have very few work propositions to make choreographies. I find that for making dance you have the top tier – this is like Kylián and friends – and they make the majority of the dance works.

They are all old men, and I am not.

Hammered out the choreography
Mindaugas (Minda) Bruzas, Vilnius

I thought it would be cool to do a showcase, so I called up some friends and invited them to be part of it with me and they were like, 'yeah, we can do this'. It was about two months before the show that I called them, and then a week later I hammered out the choreography on my own.

I started nagging everyone to gather, and as it happened not everyone could gather at the same time, so the first time we got together was a week before the show. We spent one day learning the choreography and we had three of the seven people at the rehearsal, then the next day we had four of the seven people there, two days before the show there were three people who had not ever been to the rehearsals. Then two more people came and they had to learn the material.

We finished the show, went to the pre-selection and won the whole show with our makeshift team. We won the whole championship, so it was pretty dope.

A ball
Laura Lohi, Malmö

In making work I have been involved in some strange tasks.

One of the ones that didn't end up being on stage was where we had to treat another person as an object. For example, one of us would be a ball, and you would have to be as authentic and as real as a ball would be – don't be a representation of a ball, but *be* a ball. Other people would kick, throw or bounce the ball, things that you would normally do with a ball.

We did this task in many different ways, and it became something super weird.

Tony Antanas Ceponis, Vilnius We were dancing in black and white and there were neon lights, and I mean we were not as good as *America's Got Talent*, but it was the very first showcase that I did so it is really stuck in my head.

'Try it like this?'
Modjgan Hashemian, Berlin

While I was studying dance I realised that I liked to create.

Every time the teachers would make choreographies I would watch them and think, 'could you do it like this? Or maybe we could try it like this?'

I was always taking the position of the choreographer.

Sit in the sun
Cher Geurtze, Copenhagen

Inspiration for the work I was making was coming from what was on the street, what was happening out in the world. I was studying at a conservatory situated on the edge of a park, and all the homeless would come in the morning to sit in the sun along the edge of the park. I found it always interesting to talk to them. So many of the homeless people's stories and dialogues came into my choreography.

I was playing
Anamet Magven, Læsø

I liked to be very physical, and I liked the 'doing' of the dancing. I would choose pieces of music and then through that kind of improvise. Without even really knowing what I was doing, I was playing. Then from there I moved into forming movement and structure more, and building the dance from the beginning.

A statement
Atte Herd, Rovaniemi

Right now I am working on a duet for two women around the concept of the moment of falling in love.

I know that theme of love is very common in dance works, and it has been done so many times, and so many times better than what I am capable of. But what inspires me is the exact moment of realisation of the 'one' when falling in love, which is a very special moment to me.

I know that the decision of having two women makes it kind of a statement, but there's a reason for that. This is because in Rovaniemi, there are just really not many male dancers. It's basically just me, and I don't want to dance in my own work, I needed to see it from the outside.

A whole world
Vitaly Kim, St Petersburg

The first time that I picked up a camera was seven years ago. I wanted to film my oldest son, after he had just been born.

In that moment where I picked up the camera and began recording, I realised that I wanted to do film with movement. In this moment I realised that through the camera frame I saw a whole world, I saw the film that I really wanted to make. I forgot about everything else around me.

With my friends
Cher Geurtze, Copenhagen

I was getting into performance, on the street and in the site-specific environment. This was back in the time of the hippies, so people were very adamant about getting out there, and also using performance for political statements.

So when I got to the dance conservatory in Boston to begin my studies, I was already at that state of mind in relation to performance and the work I wanted to do. Unfortunately the dance conservatory was about 30 years behind the times. I went, 'oh my God!', it was an enormous conflict for me.

I wanted to take the dance classes, but at the same time I wanted to produce my own work, I wanted to be showing my work, I wanted to be cooperating with jazz musicians who were next door at Berkeley College.

So what happened was that I got together a group of dance students who had the same kind of feelings. Almost every day after our technique classes, which finished at 5 or 6p.m., we would find a studio and work together, and began to produce our own work.

So there I was at 18 years old, with a small company, together with my friends. We were beginning to book shows at the local schools. I would get up at 5a.m. to call everyone up, to say 'are you up?', we would meet and go to a school to perform at 8a.m.. It was not something that was looked at positively from the conservatory until later. When I graduated, and those at the conservatory saw my portfolio they were like, 'hmmm, what have you been doing?'

A social body
Mart Kangaro, Tallinn

I started to hang out more with choreographers who are so-called conceptualists. I became part of that late nineties early zeroes generation in Europe who maybe went into the essence of movement.

The question of the body within dancing was very much in my mind. I was questioning, is it just a physical, anatomical body or is it a social body?

Working with the body became more important to me than working with the movement. When working with the social body, movement was part of it as a voice and the words we utter.

He was late
Anna Solakius, Lund

To create a show, you normally dance four or five songs – a tango, a waltz, or tango waltz, a miloga and maybe sometimes a dance to alternative music.

In my mind it is nice to have something that is improvised, so you get the individuality of the dancers, and also something that is choreographed, where you can put some different elements and special things to the music. I think a lot depends on who it is that you're going to make the choreography with, and what the theme is. Maybe sometimes it's just that you love a particular song, and you want to choreograph to it, or you have some moves that you would like to add into a choreography, or you just want to do a move with a particular partner because he does it very well. It totally depends.

There was one time that I finished a choreography without my partner because he was late and we had a tough time schedule, so I didn't bother to wait for him, I just finished it. We had set some of the movements at the start, and I just continued the dance. By the time he had arrived, I had finished.

But different dancers make choreography differently. One of the partners I had was very visual and he could see a whole choreography in his mind. For me, it is more about the feeling, as in 'this doesn't feel very good, I would rather move like this instead'.

But in my collaborations now, I am more equal with my partner in creating choreography. However, I find it challenging as a follower because, of course, I don't have the same vocabulary as the leader. Maybe I know what I want to do, but I can't lead it.

Eyes focused
Niina Vahtola, Oulu

I remember making a particular choreography for a group of kids with the idea that you had to keep your eyes focused to the audience at all times, even if you're facing the back, you still had to try to keep your eyes on the audience. It was a piece that had been made for adults originally. It was so hilarious that I tried to do that with the children. Of course it didn't work and it was awful, because they didn't have the same focus as the adults.

Four letters
Vadim Kasparov, St Petersburg

To be honest I didn't have any plans to make a dance festival, I didn't have any ideas about presenting dance companies, I just didn't have this experience. The Open Look Dance Festival started in 1999, 18 years ago now.

It started because a colleague in the United States called me up to tell me that an American dance company was coming to St Petersburg. Apparently the company was having difficulties with the people who were supposed to take care of the company when they would be in Russia, they were not answering very quickly and the American dance company had no information.

My colleague was worried, and I said, 'well, how can I help?'

She said, 'could you take control of this?'

I said, 'no problem' and that was it.

I asked the company to send me their technical requirements, I didn't understand any of it, but I could see what they needed. It was two weeks before they arrived, and I thought we better quickly promote that the company was going to be here, and this was before social media was really popular. So I thought 'what is popular at the moment in Russia? American collaboration!', so I called it 'American–Russian Summer Dance Workshop'. I wrote this in English on the posters because that used to always make people think 'wow, what is that?' I promoted it as a workshop and performance in one package.

Then I went to the American Embassy and told them that this was happening, they gave me $900 for the event. With this money I rented the theatre, I got the accommodation for a week for the company, so everything was covered. The company came, they had full houses and really good workshops.

So this first festival was like an accident, and during this time the newspapers kept coming to me asking what was going on? I thought that maybe I was onto something, that I could do something with this and make it something official – a festival! I started to think about what to call this festival, a contemporary dance festival. I thought 'what is the biggest problem here in Russia?', and it was that most of the people, especially professional dance people, close their eyes to things that are different. I wanted them to open their eyes, to see what was around. I thought 'open eyes' sounded no good, then I thought 'open look' – four letters, four letters, this is good. Open Look Dance Festival.

The festival is all about diversity, diversity of styles, of techniques, of ideas, everything. Step by step we developed this. When I started I was not thinking about the festival in 10 years or 20 years. I feel like we have just established some roots.

Five ghetto-blasters
Cher Geurtze, Copenhagen

My first goal in Copenhagen was to make a major performance at the Town Hall. It involved dance sequences, speaking sequences and five ghetto-blasters that the dancers had spread out in the space. We did an hour's performance there, for a week.

Hidden war
Vita Khlopova, Moscow

Over the last couple of years I have created a website for contemporary dance here in Russia. It started when I was in Paris and I made my own personal blog in WordPress. I called it *No fixed points*, so this name has been with me for quite some time.

The *No fixed points* blog has been going in its current form for nine months. It is a site in Russian, where you can know more about the work of contemporary dance choreographers and those who have influenced contemporary dance all around the world. At the same time I post things on the blog to keep people up to date with what is happening in the dance scene in Russia.

I wanted to do this because I was sick of information being incorrect. For example, there is a Wikipedia article in Russian about Merce Cunningham, and it was written there for several years that 'Merce Cunningham was a student of Mary Wigman'. Wikipedia pages can be amended, so I changed it to 'Merce Cunningham was a student of Martha Graham'. The next day it was changed back to Mary Wigman! I was like why? Who is doing this? And for about one year I had this hidden war with a person over this.

So now I have created this blog for people in Russia who want to know more about contemporary dance.

Atoms and space
Vitaly Kim, St Petersburg

Now I'm working on a new film, and in this the dancers and I are exploring the idea of touching, because I think touch can communicate a lot of information. We are thinking about what it is like when you touch someone you love, someone you work with, someone you don't know?

Also the film is about the process of non-touching, for example if you are in a crowded place you just move to your destination, and you don't want to touch people, and people don't want to touch you.

I've also thought about kids touching, touch is one way that they explore the world, and it is kind of their way of understanding the world to gather more information. My son, Leon, he doesn't speak, but he explores the world by touching. So Leon's behaviour has inspired me to make this film. My older son watched a documentary about touching, and it was all about atoms and space and there was something about how when we touch we are not really touching each other. When he heard this he almost cried and said, 'but I want to touch you!'

Footprints
Jo Parkes, Berlin

I made a video work with women in the refugee centre called *Mother*, which is really just about being a mum. I wanted to share something of my life, because when I knock on these women's doors they open it up and I see their whole world. I see their bed, I see their table, I see their husband in his pyjamas, and you know I thought they have to know something about me.

I brought in footprints of my children, from when they were babies, to show the women involved in the project. I would say to them, 'I have two sons'.

We started to dance around our experiences of motherhood. We decided then to make the film specifically about the idea of motherhood. I also think that there is something about the process of making something about perspectives for the future. That the process of being involved in this dance project and in making this film is about trying to give impulses or trying to think about 'what will happen now?' beyond the refugee centre, beyond the situations they find themselves in right now.

4
Performing

Reindeer farm
Anni Pilhjarta, Rovaniemi

Here in Rovaniemi, we don't have many performance venues. We had one production where we actually performed in a nightclub. That was interesting because we didn't really have a stage to dance on, but in a nightclub you have this dance area, so we danced there and the audience were all around us.

We also have performances for tourists, and they can take place in a reindeer farm. There's just one right outside the centre from Rimpparemmi, maybe 10 km away. It's an open-air building with a fireplace inside, with a small floor built outside, and that's where we danced. The reindeer are just behind the fences watching us dance, and of course, tourists too.

I think that's just fun, and think it is amazing that I get paid to dance next to reindeers.

Awful to perform
Alexa Wilson, Berlin

With my favourite work to perform, *Weg: A-way*, I have had the best performance of my career and the worst performance of my career.

The worst performance was certainly the day after my grandmother died, and so it was just awful to perform. I was performing this in the city where she was from, so it was hard, really hard.

Modjgan Hashemian, Berlin Shortly before my father died he came to one of my performances and he gave me peace. He said to me, 'I think you are absolutely right, and you did the right thing to go in this direction'.

A whole unit
Özen Erdinc, Malmö

Malmö City Theatre Company often used kids in their big productions. My first production was the first autumn I had started ballet school, and we had only started with pliés and relevés, but they needed a lot of kids for Bournonville's *Napoli*.

I remember being on stage, and the director and the assistant choreographer instructing the kids, telling us where to run and where to look. I was so amazed by the experience. We had a little dance in it, but it was more about being on stage as a whole unit. That memory remains deeply rooted in my heart and mind, I will never forget it.

Living in the mountains
Wioletta Milczuk, Grodzisk Mazowiecki

My favourite dance to perform is the Jurgów i Góralski. Even though I am from Western Poland I really like the dances from Southern Poland, like the Podhale region or the Spisz region. I think I like these sorts of dances because they are almost acrobatic, with many complicated movements.

Because I like dances like this it makes me think that in my previous life I might have been a highlander living in the mountains!

Maybe that is why I like these dances!

B Boy 'something something'
Mindaugas (Minda) Bruzas, Vilnius

My full name is Mindaugas, but people call me Minda.

When B Boys dance we never use our full names, we are always called B Boy 'something something'. So when you sign up for contests you're asked for your first name and last name, and I'll write B Boy 'M'.

It's easier like that.

If no one asked a question you were done for
Alexa Wilson, Berlin

Oracle was a performance that I always found to be the most nerve-wracking performance to do because essentially I started the performance with the statement: 'I am going to be here, you can ask me a question and I am going to respond to you in performance' and it might be interactive, or not.

In some contexts I just did one-on-one questioning and I've discovered that different cultures have really different responses to that approach. New York loved it and thought it was hilarious. They were just like 'it's serious, but it's not that serious, like she's an oracle' and they were going along with it. I think they found it refreshing so they just went with it, whereas in Europe, and especially in Berlin, it is so hard to get a laugh out of anybody! You feel like it is a feat when it happens! But it is more like a subtle appreciation, and I have come to realise that. Austria and Germany, even if they are quiet it doesn't mean they are not enjoying it. They might be getting a lot out of it even if they are sitting back looking like they don't want you to be there. That's quite hard, but I think it helps you grow as a performer.

I did the *Oracle* at Art Space in Auckland when I returned to New Zealand. The very first question was a deep question asked by a personal friend. Usually when I am overseas I wouldn't go straight into a dark, deep answer, I would make a more light response to ease in. But I thought, 'no, Auckland can handle this', this was my home and it went really serious. It was dealing with death, and the loss of loved ones, and I knew that I had the support of the community to go there. I think the performances succeeded because they were open to failure, because if no one asked a question you were done for. That I think is why it made it exciting for the audience, it was like 'what is she going to do now?'

Red lipstick
Magdalena Jankowski, Otrebusy

I remember the first time I did my makeup for a performance the director came over to me and said, 'you cannot do your eyes like this because you look like you are cross-eyed'. She told me how to fix it, she told me how to do it so it looked good. I learnt that I had to darken my eyebrows because they are too light and that red lipstick is a must.

The false lashes were something I had to do a couple of times to get the hang of. I quickly had to learn to open my eye after sticking the lash on, so my eyelids didn't stick together! Another thing I had to practice was how to use the fake hair, and how to attach it correctly. Early on I got the fake hair and I went home and practised for hours.

Like a kid
Moa Westerlund, Stockholm

When my grandmother saw me dance, she said to me, 'you dance like when you were a child'.

I was like, 'did nothing happen? Really? I educate myself, I go through all this practice and I look the same as I did when I was a kid?'

Anamet Magven, Læsø I worked with a horse whisperer and I made a choreography with his horses. He taught me with two or three horses, we built up a relationship and language.

But when my grandmother said that, I believed her in some way, I think there are some certain movements or ways of moving where you move like a kid.

Stabbed me
Iwona Wojnicka, Warsaw

There came a point where I couldn't stand performing anymore. I was doing all these events, and they were sold out, but it was so boring.

I felt it literally during one performance. I had this moment on stage, where the pin on my costume came undone and stabbed me in my ribs. As this happened the lights went up and the music started, and I was like 'oh gosh!'

I thought, 'this is the end'.

This was my last performance in Butoh.

Tony Antanas Ceponis, Vilnius When I was a small kid I just wanted to run around. I didn't want to do steps that the dance teachers told me to do.

Wioletta Milczuk, Otrebusy I've performed for royal families and the Pope. They are unforgettable concerts, but if a performance takes place in my hometown or when my friends and family come to watch, it is special.

Majia Rantanen, Espoo At first dancing was a total mystery to me, how to get my extremities to move at the right time in the right direction, and also co-ordinate of all four limbs?

Pitor Zalipski, Otrebusy My two-year-old daughter will start dancing soon, and I think the younger generation will find a good road to take Polish dance.

Laura Lohi, Malmö It is not just about learning the steps, that does not seem to be enough for me anymore.

Anamet Magven, Læsø I would make some posters myself on the computer in the internet café and just put them up on the walls, and that is how I started teaching classes.

Gosia Mielech, Poznan I have my own dance company, which is more like a platform where I invite people to collaborate from different genres of art – like musicians, visual artists, painters, dancers, and composers.

Veera Lamberg, Helsinki I remember many things from when I started dance, especially the feeling of how I could really express myself.

Gosia Mielech, Poznan I think that we as humans are limitless in dance, only our mind creates limitations in movement.

Marija Kaklauskaite, Vilnius A friend of mine started dancing, so I said to her 'that's cool, can I join you?'

Modjgan Hashemian, Berlin The beauty of when I go to different places where I don't speak the language – like Arabic when I work in Baghdad – we talk through movement and we talk through dance.

Rash Sensei, Copenhagen Sometimes people call me Rash Titan, because when I am doing some workshops, performances or battles I look like a Titan.

Scandalous
Mart Kangaro, Tallinn

My most scandalous or most controversial performance was when I left the Opera 2001. I staged a performance for the ballet and it was meant to be one short performance out of five works shown in the evening.

It was politically a very loaded time at the opera, the artistic director was to be replaced and a lot of dancers left. I thought really that what could I do in this context of opera? What can I offer?

I decided to do a piece about the dancers. What happened was that the dancers started to talk – instead of dancing, they talked about themselves. They revealed the details, very small details about themselves to the audience.

I could see that the audience who came to see the ballet was not ready for this. Half of the audience liked it a lot, but let's say half of the audience, they left the show, and they not only left but they also reacted verbally about what they saw.

For me as a young choreographer, even though I knew that what I did was provoking, it was surprising for me that the audience couldn't adjust or was not open enough to listen to people on stage, to listen to the private stories of those dancers.

It indicated that actually we are not at all interested in who these people, the dancers, are and that we kind of take them as instruments who are there just to fulfil this illusion of a dance performance.

A spotlight
Özen Erdinc, Malmö

We had a tour to Turku with a work called *Minus 7*.

In *Minus 7* there was a final section called *Dance with the Audience*, and we actually danced with the audience. We would get audience members to come up on stage and dance to the music of Dean Martin, songs like *Somewhere Over The Rainbow*. Once we had danced with the audience and they had left the stage, only the dancers were left. For the last bars of the music, there would be a spotlight on each dancer, and we were just moving to the song *Sway* by Dean Martin.

At this point of the performance you're so out of breath, because it was a very physically heavy piece, like you're gut was going to come out, and you're holding hands with the other dancers.

I remember watching the lights, and you have the sensation of your other colleagues, and those in the wings around you. In one of those moments, I remember thinking that I was so thankful and happy to be there. I just wanted to embrace it and I just never wanted it to end.

An email
Njara Rasolo, Helsinki

When I arrived in Helsinki I saw that an ethnic dance competition was coming up, and the winner would get 3000 euros. So I thought I would do it.

I danced, and I really killed myself on that stage, and I think the people appreciated it.

Then I didn't win anything.

I was disappointed, but then the next day the director of an art museum who was in the audience wrote an email to me and said, 'I need you for an upcoming event'. After that, word got around and people would call me up and say, 'there is this event, can you dance at it?' and it just opened things up, just from a competition that I lost.

Prostitute reindeer
Atte Herd, Rovaniemi

The premiere of a dance piece called *Sahara* is memorable for me.

As the audience came in I was on stage pushing a shopping cart, with the sign 'open' on it. I was wearing a military helmet with candles on it, with a ladies' fur coat and really high-heeled shoes. I was playing the character of a 'prostitute reindeer', as our choreographer playfully called the role. I would then go off the stage after the audience had been seated.

The next character that I played was like a CEO, someone who was above everyone, wearing a really nice suit. This then led to the next part of the show where as the CEO I had to force everyone to do things, and I had to take control of the whole situation, which was really difficult for me. At that point, I was still kind of shy so I had to really work on my confidence. I had to tell myself that I could do it.

However, something happened during the premiere, and I just walked on stage and owned the fucking performance from there on.

Shaved my head
Satoshi Kudo, Stockholm

I performed in Sidi Larbi Cherkaoui's *Sutra* with the Shaolin monks. I even shaved my head for the *Sutra* performances.

Play fighting
Atte Herd, Rovaniemi

My first performance memory is from when I was about six years old.

There was this one dance that my mum choreographed. All the boys were playing the role of Batman and the girls were cast as pirates. I don't exactly remember much of it, but the dance started off with the Batman theme song from the '60s TV series, with us just running across the stage back and forth play fighting on stage, with oddly, the Superman pose at one point, where one fist is in the air.

The pirates then came in and we fought. I think the pirates won because they were girls and we couldn't hit them.

One shoe
Magdalena Jankowski, Otrebusy

Sometimes I have to do a quick change in three minutes between dances. In those three minutes everything has to change – your shoes and clothing. There are no zippers, everything has to be tied. Often the girls wear three different skirts, there is the blouse and then the over dress. The necklaces have to change, and then you have to fix your hair.

Sometimes there are three people helping you with the change. Someone is doing your right foot while the other is doing the left foot, and you are trying to change your top. Sometimes people forget one shoe and have to go onstage with one bare foot!

Share the vibe
Marija Kaklauskaite, Vilnius

There is competing and then there is dancing in circles. For dancing in circles there is no competition; people just go into the circle and share the vibe. In the circle you connect with people, you see them and they see you. Dancing

Marija Kaklauskaite, Vilnius For me my favourite style is b-boying, or breaking, because it requires a little more strength.

in the circle is not about spectating, it is about being part of the group and the energy.

Competing is more about *my* best, and showing that. In either situation it is about showing how my body feels, is my body scared? Is it impressed? Is it happy with what I am doing? It is about the communication. I want people to be impressed, I want little kids to look at me and go 'wow, I want to be like you!'

I like the breaking because it gives me doubts; I have a challenge with it. I like dancing with the boys, most of our trainers are men, it doesn't bother me and if anything it pushes me more because I see what they can do and I want to match it and do more than the boys.

Proper ballet floor
Elwira Piorun, Warsaw

In the 1980s I joined the Polish National Ballet, but it was time where there was a state war in Poland so we were living in absolute poverty due to the political regime.

Magdalena Zalipska, Otrebusy Performing at the Polish Woodstock Festivals is memorable for me. Performing at 2a.m., with 500,000 people watching and screaming 'we love Mazowsze Dance Ensemble!' is amazing.

However, the good thing at this time was that many famous choreographers were coming here to work with us, and they wanted to come here, even though there was no money to pay them. So we were dancing works by people like Balanchine and Neumeier, all the big names in ballet at that time, but we didn't have anything.

Neumeier had to bring everything for the performance himself – the proper ballet floor, he brought that. He also had to bring the lycra for the costumes.

Playing animals
Magdalena Zalipska, Otrebusy

The first performance that I was involved with was a typical children's performance, all the kids were playing animals or other funny characters. I think I was nine years old. I remember feeling very stressed, but it was like motivating stress though.

A good belt
Nina Hoikma, Rovaniemi

I had an embarrassing moment in a show last spring. I was dancing a ballet piece and then a flamenco piece. I danced the ballet piece, and then had one dance in between for a quick change into my flamenco costume. It was very quick, and my belt wasn't on correctly.

So when I was doing the stamping with my feet in the flamenco, I felt my trousers going down.

It was terrible.

The trousers slipped further, and I just picked them up and carried on dancing. I am sure it felt more dramatic for me than it appeared to be to the audience, and some of the audience members didn't even notice, but I knew it had happened and couldn't think about anything else while I danced.

I know I need a good belt next time.

Borders were opened
Vytis Jankauskas, Vilnius

In 1986 a group of friends and I became the breakdance champions of the former Soviet Union.

Anna Paś, Otrebusy I consider the performances to be the most stressful thing, but also the most rewarding thing, about training.

88   Dance, Diversity and Difference

Rash Sensei, Copenhagen We perform in a lot of places, in the refugee camp, at Tivoli, the Roskilde Festival and in collaboration with the Red Cross in different asylum centres around Denmark.

I also performed in nightclubs, dancing on the stage, and that was my first acquaintance with performing – breakdancing and club dancing. So breakdancing taught to me that dance could be a powerful language.

Only after Lithuania gained independence in 1990 and the borders were opened did I start to discover and perform contemporary dance.

Remain silent
Rash Sensei, Copenhagen

The first performance I did with my crew was in the Congo. We were talking about politics and this performance was talking about things going on in the news, specific things going on in the Congo and the political situation at the time.

People – the government – did not want us to continue because of what we were speaking about through our performance. A lot of dancers in the crew, a lot of friends, did not continue to dance because of this pressure to remain silent.

But the three of us that started the crew, we continued.

The trigger
Gosia Mielech, Poznań

We have this crazy censorship in Poland right now. It is happening all over the country, it is getting more and more popular to ban performances, and it is almost starting to become routine nowadays.

It makes me want to push the boundaries, to challenge people. I mean not being especially provocative but to pull the trigger in people's mind so they will start to think more independently. I mean we have to, someone has to do it, and I see it as an artist's responsibility to touch taboo subjects.

'Now I know'
Piotr Zalipski, Otrebusy

A memorable performance for me was the first time I performed for my grandmother. This was when I was with Śląsk Dance Group, about 17 years ago. After my performance she came up to me and said, 'now I know why you need to dance'.

'Why not smile yourself?'
Maija Rantanen, Espoo

To see myself dancing on a video was a shock. I thought I was moving beautifully. I was not. I looked like a bag of sand, a sullen bag of sand. This is when I had a strong revelation.

A new woman joined our class. She was pretty and always smiling. I felt a pang of jealousy. I thought, 'the teacher must like her more than the rest of us'.

Then an idea struck me, 'why not smile yourself? It is allowed'.

I started smiling when I danced and from that moment on I noticed how much I liked the mirrors in dance classes. All the people in the class looked beautiful in them. There is the traditional image of a dancer being a beautiful, thin, young woman, but all women can and should dance, no matter their size.

Maija Rantanen, Espoo An ageing body sets its limits. I don't like jumps or quick turns. But I find I am free to cheat and stick to my abilities. I have realised that you don't have to spin every time all the others spin.

Theatre atmosphere
Moa Westerlund, Stockholm

As a child it was a very nice experience to be in a theatre surrounded by professional dancers, singers and actors. I still remember the sound of the orchestra playing before the performance, the opera singers warming up their voices and the dancers taking class. The theatre atmosphere, and this work that goes on before the performance, it is magical.

Moa Westerlund, Stockholm I find that there is a liberating feeling with improvisation.

In nirvana
Susanne Frederiksen, Copenhagen

I did a class with Bill Luther, we were in a theatre, there was a tabla player playing great rhythms, and we were doing triplets across the floor. I just felt like I was flying. There was no effort.

I have a lot of these dancing moments, when things just fall into place.

I have also seen a lot of students when they experience this moment of 'wow! What happened there?' It is something where the body and mind click and you are just there in that moment, and nothing else matters. You just take off, you are so integrated, and it must be like being in nirvana. It's like an encounter with a higher consciousness.

Little laughs
Njara Rasolo, Helsinki

The company I was in, *Afro-Rap*, performed mixed street dance, contemporary dance and traditional dances from Madagascar.

One day there was a dance festival in Madagascar and a French producer was watching. Right after our performance he came to our lodge and told us 'I am going to invite you to France for my festival', like right away, right there. We were all like 'wow!'

That was in 2001, and *Afro-Rap* was invited to this French festival, and at that festival there happened to be another producer from Paris watching this. Then from there they were interested to work with us, and we created a tour in Europe, from 2002 to 2005.

Somehow we were just one of the few African dance companies that had made it that far, especially through street dance. So we were always pushing that part of our identity as Africans and as Madagasi, to put that on the stage, rather than just trying to do cool street dance moves on a theatre stage. So we were really talking about every day life in Madagascar, the fun, the drama, having little laughs here and there. I guess in each dance festival we went to our touch was a bit different. Because other companies were very technical, and we were more like 'let's cool down a little bit'.

Most beautiful Bachata
Oxana Bellamy, Helsinki

I was about to leave a pub once and a man came up to me and said, 'please don't leave, the Bachata is coming up soon, and I would like to dance the Bachata with you'.

I knew he was a good dancer, so I didn't leave, and that night I experienced perhaps the most beautiful Bachata in my life.

This man, I think he was from Cuba, he asked me, 'where do you come from?'

I said, 'from Russia'.

He said, 'I thought so, please carry on dancing, keep going'. I was very proud.

White piece of material
Liva Zorgenfreija, Riga

I was dancing the premiere of a dance where I had a solo. It was super stressful, with a costume change in less than three minutes beforehand.

In Latvian dance there are many pieces of clothing to put on. I had four people helping me, and I quickly rushed out onto the stage while the stage was still dark. Once I was on stage I realised that my waistcoat was still open, because it was still dark I quickly buttoned it up. Then I realised that my cuffs were open, so I was closing those as the lights came up. Then at the very beginning of the dance my partner was lifting me and the heel of my shoe ripped a part of my skirt off!

For the whole dance there was this white piece of material from the skirt getting in the way of my dancing. Also, I had ribbons in my braids and those fell off as well!

I cried after that performance, and even though it was not my fault it was upsetting, because I thought it was going to go well. I was ready for the dance, and I had practised and rehearsed a lot.

It was just terrible, but I am getting over it slowly!

Always food
Jo Parkes, Berlin

Every ten weeks the artistic teams working in the refugee accommodation centres change. When this change happens there is what we call 'dance parties' or 'get togethers' and the people can share what they have done in the workshops with us.

This often entails everyone dancing with the artists who have facilitated workshops, and everyone in the accommodation centre, but also the wider neighbourhood is invited. We all dance together. So there is this facilitated dance and then there is always food at the end.

Crying like a baby
Njara Rasolo, Helsinki

When my crew and I lost a competition in Ghana it was broadcast live on TV. The way we lost was not cool. The Kenyans were before us, and they used some powder on the stage. The producer forgot to clean the stage after this, so we went on stage and we fell in all of our flips and tricks.

So we lost.

Afterwards I was crying like a baby behind the stage. The cameras were filming me, and then I had to go on stage and talk to the audience. I went on stage and I pulled myself together. As I walked out on the stage people started clapping, really clapping. The judges stood up, they were clapping and crying.

I said, 'today we lost at the final, and we thank you guys for this magnificent journey, but we would like to tell you that this is not our end, it is our beginning'.

Now, when I go back to Tanzania I remind the boys who I danced with 'remember that time…'.

There are ups and downs, but we are still here, because we are the actors of this culture and we need to make the people believe that we can help, while keeping the hip hop philosophy of peace, love and unity. Period.

32 years
Krysztof Fijak, Otrebusy

I feel a little nervous before going on stage, but I think, 'I have to do it'. I think about performing each time like it is the first time I am going on stage. I like it, it is my life. I try to do it the best I can. I hope I can continue dancing, but I have been dancing with Mazowsze Dance Ensemble for 32 years. I don't think about stopping dancing too much. Some days I wake up and think, 'maybe that is enough, it's time to retire', but then other days I think, 'no, I can keep going'.

This artist identity
Veera Lamberg, Helsinki

I am still a performer, and want to perform. My challenge is to try to keep this performing going in my life. It is a difficult thing to make a living from dancing, so I have many options and I can combine things – teaching, performing, choreographing, writing – but it is challenging for me because I have to be able to train myself as well, and it can be a difficult thing to balance this.

It is surprisingly difficult to have this artist identity and at the same time try to find a way to do all the things you need to do to make a living in dance. I feel that sometimes people quickly assume that you just do one thing. For example, they see you teach and then they think you don't dance anymore. I strongly feel that I use my dance expertise in everything I do, and I don't leave it behind when I do different things.

Dancing 'father'
Petezis Studens, Riga

A strong memory of dancing for me was performing in a 'fathers' and 'sons' dance. I was one of the 'sons', one of the small ones. I thought those that were the 'fathers' were big grown men, but in reality they were just teenagers, like 15 or 16 years old.

When I performed this dance it must have been 1994, and my actual father was on a business trip to Dublin in Ireland at the time, I had not seen him for a while, and in this dance we called these older guys we were dancing with our 'fathers'. I got quite attached to the guy who was my dancing 'father', maybe I was missing my own!

But then there was one rehearsal where there was a change to our 'fathers', and the 'father' we danced with changed, we got a new 'father' to dance with. This was a bit of a struggle for me to have a new dancing 'father'!

A few days after this my real father came back from Ireland and I said to him, 'father, father! I have a new father!'

You know, my father had been away for a few weeks, and he looks at my mother like 'what is going on?!'

Santa Claus Village
Helmi Järvensivu, Rovaniemi

Until I moved to Lapland, Santa Claus and the Christmas season had never really been a big thing for me. But ever since I started working at Rimparemmi, I realise that Santa Claus is a mega thing here, and Christmas practically lasts the entire year.

We have had some performances at the Santa Claus Village in the Arctic Circle, and performing in the Arctic Circle with Santa Claus is a pretty special moment. There are thousands of tourists and they are all so excited about Christmas.

Ten dances
Ella Gröndahl, Oulu

There was one performance I did where I was one of the Cheshire Cats from *Alice in Wonderland*. It was a spring performance, and my friends who were also Cheshire Cats and I thought that there was going to be a break in between the first ten dances and the second ten dances. We thought that we would have the time to change our clothes and get ready.

But I remember that someone said, 'no, there's not the break!'

We were the 11th dance, and we started panicking. We got ready so quickly and ran on stage. It was so fun!

I thought, 'this is what it's like to be a dancer!'

Everything was in a hurry and it was a bit of a panic, but when I got onto stage, I was really excited and felt that I was really a dancer now – 'so this is what it really feels like!'

Classic stockings
Anna Solakius, Lund

One of the problems that can happen when you are performing tango and you are the follower is that your heel can get stuck in your dress during a performance.

Now I remember the worst time this happened to me was during one of my first performances.

I had these classic stockings on, skin-coloured fishnets. I and my partner had danced one dance, and we were just about to do our first new choreography. We were waiting to go on stage and I felt that my dress got stuck in the stockings, but I didn't really know how, because we hadn't even started dancing yet. I didn't know how bad it was. I thought 'can I dance with it like this, or should I remove the stockings?'

I quickly went and took the stockings off, as I didn't know if the dress was over my butt or something. Taking off the stockings was the only way I was able to relax and dance.

Very wavy
Niina Vahtola, Oulu

When I was nine or ten years old, I was performing a polonaise dance. We had these beautiful white skirts and pale blue tops, and I just loved the movements in this dance.

There was a particular movement in the dance where we had to flow our hands forward and backwards, while doing a sequence with our feet. The movement was very wavy, and I liked that. At the same time the music was very sharp. I was very confident with this movement.

Insane, or drunk
Katerina Urbanovich, St Petersburg

When I told my friends, 'I do contemporary dance', they asked, 'what does it look like? Is it like salsa? Do you dance with a partner?'

Özen Erdinc, Malmö The disco on the boat crossing the Baltic was a chance for me to talk and bond with my classmates, boys and girls, outside of school.

I try to explain to them that sometimes we do performances that are based a bit on Butoh, but also experimental theatre, and we do this maybe in a gallery or in the street, and we do live performances and make films. When we perform in the street people often wonder what we are doing. Some people think maybe we are insane, or drunk. Often people will call the police.

Sometimes we get permission to perform in public from the government organisations. Sometimes if we know the street or the museum and we know if will be okay and safe, we do it. Sometimes we have an idea, like to make a performance on the subway, but for that we'd have to ask for permission from the city government and we might not get it.

A mosquito
Simone Höckner, Malmö

I remember the first performance I did was not a dance performance, but an opera. I think it was *Faust*, and there was a lot of us children from the ballet school in the performance.

While we were doing some of the moves, one of the directors pointed at me, and instructed me to come forward on the stage. I was playing the role of a mosquito, and I remember this because I was very embarrassed about the role.

But I felt at home in the theatre. The opera singers would always come over to greet us and there was no hierarchy that I could feel. The dancers would always talk to us when we went backstage and they knew us by name. This made us kids feel important, like we were one of them.

Humanity
Veera Lamberg, Helsinki

What I feel when I dance is some kind of purpose, a sense of expressing something. I really enjoy the feeling that I can control what I am doing. That everything kind of makes sense in that moment. I also enjoy challenging myself, trying to do things that are difficult, and somehow try to get better and better.

For me dancing is becoming more about humanity, because the politics in Finland at the moment is all about money and values that I don't necessarily appreciate so much. So I think it is beautiful to watch people move and dance, and it really makes sense that we are here as human beings, and as humans who *really* feel something.

I remember the feeling when you really think that you are doing something important for yourself and hopefully for others, the feeling when you are performing that you are really on the edge but you still manage to keep it together.

Went wild
Jo Parkes, Berlin

For my work On tradition I made 12 video portraits, about 12 people who live and work in the shops on a street in Berlin called Badstraße. These people come from all over the world – Lebanon, Turkey, Germany, Iraq, the Gaza Strip, South Korea and Pakistan. The questions I asked them were things like, 'what do you do that your parents did before you?', 'how do you do it differently?' and 'how do your children do it differently?'

The films are between two and a half and seven and a half minutes long, and when the films were finished they were installed in the participants' shop windows for two weeks. The films were played from 11a.m. to 7p.m. every day and there were headphones wired outside so people passing by could listen to the audio.

When I was doing the interviews with the 12 people I was a bit cheeky, and I asked them what their best dance moment was. I was interested to know how things are passed through the body, rituals and traditions, how they are handed down through the body. Spontaneously in the first interview I said, 'what is the best dance you have had in your life?'

The man I was talking to was a wonderful Pakistani man who sells clothes, he's beautifully groomed, and up until that point he'd answered every question with one very short sentence. I must have asked 100 questions. But when I asked him this question he described bhangra dance. I was a bit dishonest and I pretended like I didn't know what bhangra dance was.

I said, 'could you show me what bhangra dance is?'

While he was talking to me his body language was completely still, and then we put the music on, he began dancing and he went wild. It was the most glorious moment.

Small red lights
Raivis Dzjamko, Riga

When I first started dancing I was dancing with the Opera Company here in Riga. I had never been to the Opera House before this time, and I had never been on a stage like this before.

The first time I went on the stage, it was just for a rehearsal. I recall stepping out onto the stage and everything was dark, but I could see the outline of the seats in the auditorium and could tell that all the seats were covered with red material. Looking out further into the darkness I could see that there were some small red lights out in the audience. The stage lights above and in the wings of the stage gave me stars in my eyes when I looked at them, and they were hot and bright.

Once my eyes adjusted I could really absorb the theatre. I was like 'wow! This space is like heaven!'

5
Teaching and teachers

A circle is my friend
Jo Parkes, Berlin

The women who live in the refugee centres often bring their children to the dance workshops I facilitate.

After a while I said to them 'should we go and dance together?'

My way 'in' to work with these women was to invent an English folk dance. I often start my workshops by saying, 'I come from England', I play very traditional English folk dance music and teach them my folk dance that I have made up. It is 'Jo's folk dance' and it is done in a circle.

So dancing in a circle is my friend, and I have found that social dances work well; but each group is very different.

Very proud
Piotr Zalipski, Otrebusy

I like teaching older people because they are like friends to me. My oldest student is 82 years old. I am very proud because I am teaching them about Polish culture. Many of the people I teach might be 70 or 80 years old, but they don't know anything about Polish dancing. Now there is a return to Polish dance, people are now becoming interested in what it is and how it relates to their background and lineage.

Vitaly Kim, St Petersburg I think that I don't make a lot of movements, I just make the frames, the base systems that give the dancers the tools to do more than I can do on my own.

Dancers to dance
Vitaly Kim, St Petersburg

When I started teaching I didn't have a system, I had no books to work off, so I started to make my own system of understanding movement, of expression, of impulses. Now in my company I give the dancers this system I have been working on through my own experiences. I would call this system 'acting for dancers' – I am not teaching dancers to dance, rather I am allowing them to have their own movements and break their own movement patterns.

Exploring
Anamet Magven, Læsø

I think getting into teaching was part of a process of finding out what I had to offer society. Like, what is it that I can give and where? Where is there a need? It was not that I was particularly interested in teaching or anything like that. I was just exploring.

Very particular smell
Liva Zorgenfreija, Riga

We had a dance professor who was really old, but I was only eight years old, so everyone seems old when you are that young. I was so scared of her, terrified of her, and terrified of her class every Thursday. She was very strict, not mean, just strict. As kids you'd often like to laugh and things like that in dance class, but not with her, nothing, I remember the class being very serious.

But she did teach me a lot, I remember many things from what she told us, things about how to turn out your legs, and how to move your arms the right way so it looks professional and people believe that you know what you are doing.

She had this very particular smell, not in a bad way, but I still remember her smell when she would walk by. I remember the smell and sometimes if I am somewhere and I smell something similar all of a sudden I straighten up my back.

'Sing' with your arms
Özen Erdinc, Malmö

I remember one of my teachers very well. Her name was Barbara Gray, and she was an English lady. She was so nice, and I felt safe with her. She spoke Swedish with a British accent, and I remember that as an 11 year old, hearing someone speak Swedish in such an accent was quite different.

She was my first ballet school teacher, so there was this certain respect and aura around her. She used to tell us that for people who don't know anything about classical ballet, when watching dancers from the waist down they might not know the mistakes or your turn in or turn out, but from your waist up, they will always remember your arms. So it was something that I kept in mind later on for my career too, of decorating the upper body, to really 'sing' with your arms, to distract the audience from your deficiencies, your short legs, and turn out.

'Yes I can push play for the music'
Satoshi Kudo, Stockholm

At the end of 2014 a guy called me up and said 'Satoshi, what are you doing at the beginning of next year?'

I was like, 'well, not much really'.

And he said, 'would you be able to replace our rehearsal director because she is pregnant?'

I was like 'okay, and what is this?'

He was like, 'it's with the Royal Swedish Ballet'.

I thought, 'that's not bad!'

This position was from January until May. So I started working as the rehearsal director of the Royal Swedish Ballet, and I worked with Johan Inger, Alexander Ekman, and then they wanted me to continue to the end of the year. And what was the next production? It was *Swan Lake* by Mats Ek.

I thought, 'how old was I when I first saw that performance in Japan?' I must have been just 22. I had given up on Cullberg Ballet, I had stopped going to their auditions, Cullberg had stopped doing Mats Ek's work and the company was not the same anymore. I was getting old, and I thought I have no chance to ever do anything with Mats Ek.

Then finally I met Mats. I was totally nervous, it was a big moment for me. He was so professional and so humble. I think about it now and I have worked with all of these wonderful choreographers, but if I think about it I am very emotionally attached on a personal level to Mats Ek's work. Then when I worked with him every day I was so impressed. I was amazed at how he treated the dancers, that he pushed them, but his attitude is so serious and straightforward, there are no pretentions. I was so proud. Sometimes when you look up to someone, and you think they are perfect, and then you work with them and you are let down. Then you think, 'I wish I didn't meet you'. But with Mats it was the opposite, it was just so special.

I never told him I had auditioned for Cullberg Ballet so many times, I was trying to be professional, like, 'yes, I am a professional rehearsal director, yes I can push play for the music, yes, I can write a note, yes, I can train the dancers, sure'.

It was a journey. I have to say it was a wonderful time, and Mats, who was always the one who was sweating the most in the studio, I learnt so much from him. It was the peak of my life. It was not necessary for me to go through this, but I feel that I am very lucky to work with Mats Ek after this journey, because there is something in me that was thinking 'I never got there', it was some sort of complex that was holding me back.

But after this, it was like, 'Satoshi, you are now on your own, you have nothing to hold you back'. So it gives me a lot of confidence, but also a lot of fear, because I have no excuses anymore.

'One, TWO, pow, pow!'
Susanne Frederiksen, Copenhagen

When I returned to Denmark from London I started teaching children, and also adults in evening schools.

I was teaching Graham technique, like, 'one, TWO, pow, pow!'

People were just sweating and didn't know what was going on, but I was like 'come on, work harder!'

An open mind
Gosia Mielech, Poznań

I try to be prepared when I teach class, but I am never too strict with my ideas, that's for sure. I feel that being a bit flexible helps me to stay alert while teaching, that I am listening and ready to adapt to particular circumstances. It is about going into the studio with an open mind, and by watching people I try to get the feel of what it is that they want.

Because it is all for the people I teach. I think there are certain moments where you can push your students and be demanding, but in a friendly, respectful way. But generally, what is the point in me pushing a certain idea, my way, if it is not what they need or want? It will not work, they will just get blocked!

Gosia Mielech, Poznań When you teach you can learn so much from the experience.

106   *Dance, Diversity and Difference*

Vytis Jankauskas, Vilnius When I choose dancers, besides technical things, the personality of the dancers is very important to me. We need to understand each other and speak the same language – because in the choreographic process the dancers' involvement is very important.

Big question
Vytis Jankauskas, Vilnius

When I teach I don't have one particular system. For me it is important to ask the question: what do I use as the basis for teaching today? What is the core idea I want to communicate? And I need to ask this every day that I teach, because it changes.

There is not one single truthful or right approach to teach dance, there are many different ways and approaches.

Today when people say to me, 'come and teach contemporary dance', really big questions for me are, what is contemporary dance? Which approach of the thousands is suitable?

Trolls
Simone Höckner, Malmö

Now when I teach I have taken the story my mother used to use in her teaching, about the Swedish trolls, and I use it with the five year olds in my classes.

I ask the children, 'do you think trolls exist?'

I get all sorts of answers.

Then I get my pianist to play fantasy-like music. When the children hear this, it's like magic to them, and they just enter into another world.

They leave class with big wide eyes, full off excitement and they tell their parents about the trolls in the woods. They use their whole body as they talk and show their parents what happened in the class. I can see that the parents are really happy to have this time together with their children. The children often ask their parents if there are really trolls living in the woods. There are some who reply that it is just fantasy. I don't really like that response because I'm always telling the children, 'if you think there is something in the woods, then maybe you can see it'.

I think it's really important to have this fantasy with you for your whole life, to look at the woods and think that maybe there's something there.

Red Cross
Rash Sensei, Copenhagen

Me, my brother Bob and our friend Barley were looking forward to dancing here in Copenhagen, but it was difficult of course. We live in the Næstved Asylcenter tent camp, and we were always going to the Red Cross to ask them if it is possible to find a place to practice dancing.

There was one girl who worked in the Red Cross, and she called GAME, which is a non-profit organisation working with street sports and street culture. The girl from the Red Cross sent us there, and without her making that phone call I don't think we would be where we are today. Now GAME is like it is our home, we spend all our time practising there, and GAME gave us volunteer contracts for teaching. So we teach Afro-house, breakdance and do a lot of stuff there. It gave us a base, a beginning and a community here in Copenhagen.

'I jump, you jump, we jump!'
Modjgan Hashemian, Berlin

I created a workshop that came out of a situation where one of my dancers from Iran came to Germany, and he couldn't speak German so I thought 'okay, we will do a piece where we work with language'.

Rash Sensei, Copenhagen I would like to teach kids not to just dance to be happy, but to dance to learn something, to understand themselves more. If we understand ourselves more then perhaps we can understand each other more.

I tried to teach him German through movement.

So we created a little solo about dancing and learning a language, and how does a movement feel when you say the word in Farsi, and how does the rhythm and movement change when you say it in German?

So I am trying to do this method now with kids who go into what are called Welcome Classes here in Germany, where they have to learn German. I give workshops where we dance and learn pronouns and things like that, so it is like 'I jump, you jump, we jump!'

Anamet Magven, Læsø My own teaching has been developing towards including as little talking and doing as possible, allowing then for as many reflection spaces as possible.

In-between
Anamet Magven, Læsø

We have this word in Danish – Dannelse – which does not mean education, it is more than that, kind of like life learning or development through education. I am not sure what you'd call it in English. I use this word to describe what I do, because I feel that what I do is kind of like dance development. I love to be in-between the arts and education.

Little communities
Njara Rasolo, Helsinki

When I was first in Helsinki I was kind of open to teaching everything, I was even teaching Latin dances at one point. It went really well, but then I thought,

'I have to be myself', so I now only teach African dance, Afro dance and street dance, because that's me.

I also only focus on teaching beginners.

I don't just do choreography with them, I teach them some basics of the movements, some history about the dances, and we really delve into the culture, we don't just dance. Some people use my dance classes as a workout, but they also get to be involved more in the whole experience of dance.

I like building my own community. There are other little dance communities here and there in Helsinki, studios and things, but there is rarely a collaboration between places or sharing between people in the dance communities. I notice that people don't really go to other people's dance events or performances, but me, I go everywhere! There are no boundaries for me, for me it doesn't make sense, we are all dancers and we will only get better by sharing our ideas and practices.

Danish phenomenon
Susanne Frederiksen, Copenhagen

I was teaching in places called Højskole, which are a very special Danish phenomenon. From 18 years of age people can go to study at Højskole and there are different kinds of subjects. Niels Frederik Severin Grundtvig built this idea, and originally Højskole were developed because young people were leaving the rural areas of Denmark because there was no education available to them in the area or alternatively the only option for them was that they become farmers. So the Højskole was in order to educate people, intellectually and also culturally.

I was working in the dance department of a Højskole, doing a lot of teaching, choreography and performances. But when you teach there you are part of the community, so you also do the kitchen work, and the tours around the area.

The babysitter
Veera Lamberg, Helsinki

I have been teaching ballet for adults. It is quite popular.

I offer it at this little dance school. I wanted to offer contemporary dance as well, but the owner of the school said that it could be difficult and it depends on the students. The ballet classes seem to be more popular. Most of the people in the class had some experience in ballet when they were younger, or some experience in jazz dance.

I prefer teaching adults; I don't feel like the babysitter. I find that adults listen to what I say. It is of course difficult sometimes, because I am really interested in the art form and the quality is the most important thing for me, and this way of doing it. Some people come to the classes just to get fit, so I have to adjust myself to the situation and accept why some people are there.

Friends on Facebook
Simone Höckner, Malmö

When I started teaching, my students were about the same age as I was, 15 or 16 years old.

In the class I was teaching I fell in love with one of the students. We were both 16. He was really good looking and I thought he looked beautiful.

He would always come to the front of the class. This made it hard for me to look at the other students, because I kept going to him all the time. I knew that falling in love with a student was unprofessional for a dance teacher, but I only had eyes for him. He was an actor and he did music as well. He lives in Stockholm and we're friends on Facebook now. It was my first serious relationship.

'Kill the whales!'
Volker Eisenach, Berlin

When I was teaching workshops in New Zealand for *Sacre du Printemps* there were so many mistakes that I made because I was not familiar with the culture. There is a hunting scene in *Sacre*, and I thought, 'okay, the kids are living in New Zealand, it is an island, so let's hunt whales!'

We had this class of 11-year-old kids at a school, and I was like, 'take your spears, kill the whales!'

Then in the break the teacher came up to me and said, 'just letting you know that the whale is a sacred animal, and in Maori legends there are stories of the whales'. I didn't know.

When we started back after the break I changed it to, 'let's hunt some pigs!'

Volker Eisenach, Berlin I also find that now things go full circle, I have students who say 'Volker, I want to be a professional dancer', and I'm like 'well, you better start with classical ballet!'

Your attitude
Susanne Frederiksen, Copenhagen

Teaching is teaching is teaching. Pedagogy is pedagogy.

Of course you have to be aware of who you are teaching. I have a certain way of teaching if I am working with children, with adults, with older people, with people with Parkinson's. But regardless of the group I am teaching I like to have a lot of dynamics and for it to be humorous as well.

What matters is your attitude towards the teaching, and also to have a lot of understanding. Especially when I work with the group with Parkinson's there needs to be understanding. One day they have a lot of energy and the next day none, it is unpredictable. So you just have to tune in to them, and also challenge them a bit and push them a little bit. They can do more than what we think they can do. For me it is really important to create an atmosphere of 'I can do this!' so it is a success.

I did a class with a group on Friday, and the group was for big people, people who were on special diets and they have other kinds of health issues to deal with. In this class someone said to me, 'this is the first time in a very long time I can stand on one leg and lift the other!'

And maybe what I do as a teacher is more about guiding people into things. I like to create these magical moments, where each person who is there is feeling something, like 'I am dancing, I can do this, this is wonderful and we are here together and we can support each other'. Some people have thoughts that dancing is not for them, and that it is just for certain people, there are a lot of these prejudices about it. But then people just go out there and do it, and they realise actually it is quite fun.

Street kids
Njara Rasolo, Helsinki

I met three dancers from the street, they were good, and dedicated. They invited me to where they practice, they showed me some dancing and one of them said to me, 'man, can you please stay here and be our teacher?'

I thought, 'sure, why not?'

From there we started to invite more street kids to come to the practices. We went really hard, and I trained them really well.

A jazzy move
Laura Lohi, Malmö

I will always remember this particular lady who was in one of my classes. She was very hunched, sinking down, and because Parkinson's also affects speech and expressing words I could not hear her when she spoke. I had a hard time trying to have a conversation with her before the class, I couldn't really understand her, and it looked like she had a lot of trouble just holding her posture.

But when she started moving in the class, I was so surprised because she was very quick and she moved very fast from one place to another. It really struck me that you can't judge a person based on how they initially look when they come into the class.

She was good at learning the exercises, she could take them in quickly, and again this was not the assumption I made when I first saw her. In the beginning of class we would do exercises seated, and we would focus on arm movements. Even though she had this sunken and hunched posture, she didn't seem to have any problems reaching in and out from her body. We did this toe heel movement, where we would go across the room with a toe heel step, like a jazzy move. She was totally in it!

Democratic way
Cher Geurtze, Copenhagen

I made a strategy that I would contact the principals of the local schools, have a cup of coffee with them, tell them about the idea of having a place where kids could come and dance outside of school time. But I wanted to promote it and introduce the idea within school time, and I chose the month of August to do introductory school projects.

It was a really good idea, and I have kept this strategy, to try to introduce dance in a kind of democratic way where the leader of the school, the teachers, everyone is saying, 'let's try it'.

No stress
Oxana Bellamy, Helsinki

The teacher in Cuba showed me how women should dance like women, and gave me a lot of feedback. For me this was very nice because in Finland the teachers do not correct the students so much.

I have found that my Cuban and Russian teachers are demanding; they want the students to show that this is the best student, look at him or her.

In Finland the teachers are more about keeping it as no stress, just keep dancing, it doesn't matter who you are. It is good sometimes, especially for beginners. But for people who are motivated to learn more it can get boring.

Where I come from
Jo Parkes, Berlin

After studying in America I went back to London and I started to teach. I was teaching in the East End of London, which is a very deprived community, and it resonated with me because of where I come from, where my family are from, which is also a very deprived area and an industrial community, very diverse.

In my time in the East End I think I discovered many of the themes and approaches that I am still working with ten years later. Just in terms of themes, I find myself back with the same people working with the same themes.

Now I find I am working with refugees from the Balkan region, lots from Chechnya. Then you have those arriving now who are mainly from Afghanistan, Iraq and Syria.

Choose together
Liisa Jaakonaho, Helsinki

Working with disabled people, I find I need quite a lot of structure and repetition. I have found that it is helpful to begin and end the sessions in the same way. But I also like trying to give those involved a choice, for example they bring the music to the class and we choose together from the music that they bring what we should play. I try to encourage them to do their own movement, to show their own movement, whatever it is.

But it also seems to be important that I take that role of the teacher, and sometimes it is that I say 'this is what we will do' and I will show the movement, or 'this is the warm up' – but it needs to be clear, everything needs to be clear.

When things happen that seem to work I try to pick up on them, and say things like 'wow, that is really cool, let's continue with that'.

Why should they listen to me?
Volker Eisenach, Berlin

The choreographer that was leading this afterschool dance group I was in came less and less over the period of a year. At first she was just arriving late, but then after a while she just didn't show up at all. The first day when she arrived half and hour late I said to the group, 'maybe we can start the warm up?'

I had no clue how to do it. I took over without knowing that I took over, because it was like just one step each week.

That process took a year and then I was running the dance company, this was while I was still in school, and she got paid for it. I don't mind at all, I think it is funny. I was like 17 nearly 18 years old. It took me a lot of time and a lot of detours to figure out what I was doing, and many wrong decisions. I had no professional background; I had no education in dance.

I think the biggest problem for me at that time was the rest of the group were the same age as me, and were my friends, so why should they listen to me? Like what is my knowledge, what is my right to say things or ask things?

Alexa Wilson, Berlin Braveness in performance comes from vulnerability, and embracing that vulnerability.

A telephone call
Cher Geurtze, Copenhagen

I often say to the kids I am teaching, 'when you experience something that you like, tell me. Or if you get an idea, tell me. I will try to move on it'.

One of the things that led me to say this was one afternoon I was sitting in my office and I got a telephone call from one of the young breakdancers I taught, he would have only been about 12 years old. He said, 'Cher, we really enjoyed that show we did last week, we want to do more things like that'.

I said, 'what do you mean Mohammed?'

He said, 'well Cher, if you can get more gigs … we'll do it'.

And I thought, 'wow, they do want it, and they want to do more'.

They met at training and formed a group, they got together after school and they forced him to make the phone call. So I said, 'okay, well what if we do it like this and that, would you guys want to do that?' and they were like 'yeah!'

Tango through teaching
Anna Solakius, Lund

I learnt tango through teaching. I started teaching so early, and I didn't have much knowledge of tango or teaching before I went on to teach. I was assisting, learning and teaching all at the same time, so it took me some years before I could feel relaxed as a teacher. Now I know what I am saying, not because he or she said, or that I am copying someone else, but instead because I know what I am doing.

When I started teaching it was quite stressful and very challenging, but also very interesting to see my students do something according to my words. It made me realise that it is not necessary for you to do something yourself, as in demonstrate a movement, just so that others can do it. But I feel that I can teach much easier now, I have more knowledge and I can relax in my knowledge.

Like a VIP
Niina Vahtola, Oulu

As a kid I had gatherings with my friends outside, I was always the one organising this – telling them 'now we will play this, and you do this and you do that'. It was very natural for me to do this organisation.

It got to the point that at the times that I wasn't there, my friends would persuade me to come, as they didn't know what to do. I don't know if I was good or not, but I remember being the one who taught everyone. I made choreography, of course for myself, but I taught it to my sister and our friends. I think it was a choreography that we all did, but I was the one who made all the decisions.

I remember there was this one time that I was watching the choreography from up on the balcony on the house, and they were dancing on the street below. I felt like a VIP watching the choreography from the balcony. I was giving them comments from up there, things they could improve on, saying, 'you have to put your legs together here, and you have to watch the way you do that movement, and keep your fingers there in that position'.

Verbal language
Jo Parkes, Berlin

In the dance classes with refugees I don't have interpreters, the children interpret for each other and it is mostly physical. The wonderful thing about dance in this context is that you don't need verbal language to collectively create something together. I mean not to play art forms against each other, but I think dance in this context, as a tool, is very powerful. In the dance moments, there are times where things need to be explained, but then there is always someone to do this. When you can't always explain things you have to adapt the way you make dance and how you are going to get there, and really think about it, and get away from 'I do it, you do it'.

A quick solution
Cher Geurtze, Copenhagen

When teaching I was learning by doing. There would be things like a breakdance teacher not showing up to teach, and then having to find a quick solution, it would result in me doing the teaching, or the kids doing the teaching. Through these experiences the kids were becoming trainers too.

We would have situations where we would meet for a show, several of the students wouldn't show up, but we would still do the show. We would re-rehearse the choreography, and that was an important lesson from the beginning, be flexible, never cancel, never back down, find a way.

Not ballet
Vita Khlopova, Moscow

The students I was teaching in my experimental course at the university had their exam. The subject of this exam was the history of contemporary dance in Western Europe and the United States. It was not about ballet, it was not about classical ballet, it was not even about Soviet ballet, it was not about ballet at all, not Petipa, and not even about Béjart. However, the examination jury was from the Faculty of Ballet, because there were no other dance people in the university to invite.

I made some exam questions, because in Russia students have to pass an oral exam where they are given questions to respond to – for example 'tell us about Denishawn?' There were six questions and they had to pick one randomly. Then they have around half an hour to prepare for this and they can use their own notes.

The first question a student selected was all about the forerunners of American modern dance, so Isadora Duncan, Loie Fuller and so on, and it is not me who invented this history, it is a history that has been written down many times before. So the student started talking about them, and then one of the jury said, 'okay, why are you talking about Isadora Duncan? And Josephine Baker? She is not a forerunner'.

My student didn't know what to do. Then the woman on the jury kept talking saying 'no, Josephine Baker wasn't part of this'.

The second question was all about new French dance in the '70s. This was the theme of my thesis, so I feel I know it well. One of the students starts to speak, saying that actually in France before the '70s they had no modern dance, but it was a country of classical and modern ballet, that modern dance in France was not so à la mode.

The jury said, 'who told you such stupid things?'

I put my hand up and said, 'it was me, because it is true'.

One of the professors said, 'it's not true, what about Serge Lifar?'

I was like 'he has nothing to do with it, he was neo-classical ballet, not modern dance'.

After the French new dance, the jury wanted to ask something about Maurice Béjart, I mean he is not so new, but he is someone that they know. They asked a student to tell them about Béjart. The student said, 'okay, I don't know him so well, but I will try'.

They asked, 'what Soviet stars of the Bolshoi danced in Béjart's company?'

The student replied, 'Plisetskaya and Maximova', the jury were like 'okay, good'.

Then next question they asked, 'what Grigorovich ballet was Maximova dancing in the Bolshoi School?'

I was like, 'from asking about Béjart how did you get there?'

It was the only thing they could discuss, and of course my students didn't know this, because it was not the subject of our course. The Director of the Faculty of Ballet said, 'not knowing this is a shame on all of you, I don't know what you have been doing for the past two years, and if the students don't know about this sort of thing it is a shame on you'.

I was like, 'okay, in this country, with its history, they need to know some things about ballet, but the course was not about ballet or Soviet ballet!' It was quite strange that after two years of study about the history of contemporary dance in Western Europe and the United States they are asked these sorts of questions. It was a huge scandal at the university. After this the students had to re-pass the exam, and the director re-made the questions and the questions were about Nijinsky, Plisetskaya, Fokine and so on. There was nothing from the contemporary world.

The handstand
Niina Vahtola, Oulu

I had been only dancing for half a year when the teacher told me that I was a natural teacher, and suggested that I started teaching the younger ones. I didn't know anything about folk dance, and I didn't think that I was ready. But she said that I could, so I started teaching young dancers.

At first most of the teaching methods I had were from my ballet school training, somehow I mixed what I saw and what I experienced. There have been many times over the years that I thought that I had to be a certain kind of teacher.

When I was studying at dance school, there was a choreographer who made a contemporary dance choreography for my class. She gave me a part in the dance, and I had to do a handstand. But I hurt my wrists somehow. It got to the point that I was hurting way too much, and I had to tell her that I couldn't do the movement. I apologised to her and told her she could replace me, but she told me that I didn't have to do the handstand, and asked what else I could do instead.

That was a very big moment for me, I felt like she listened to what I had to say. I think that was the moment when I felt like I wanted to be like her as a teacher.

Back to square one
Susanne Frederiksen, Copenhagen

When I was doing community projects, I started to work with a person who was in a wheelchair.

She came into my office one day and said, 'I want to dance'.

I was like 'okay'.

So I went into the studio with her, and it kind of evolved.

I got some money for her to travel to England to work with Candoco Dance Company and to get Candoco here to Denmark. I felt like I was back to square one when I started to work with people with physical disabilities, because here in Denmark the mentality is 'you're in a wheelchair, you don't dance, you can't dance'.

The first steps
Simone Höckner, Malmö

I started teaching in schools at the beginning of 1990. Dance in schools wasn't a big thing then in Sweden, and there was practically nothing in Lund. I would go out into schools, and the students took dance class once a week with me.

The first response I got from the students was, 'no, I'm not going to dance', 'why should I dance?', and 'I don't do ballet'. But I told them that dance is really broad and it wasn't just ballet.

I had many years of ballet classes myself, but I never thought of teaching them ballet. I just asked if any of them had danced at home or danced in schools during disco parties, or even when they were two years old with nappies on, moving to music – those are the first steps.

6

Family, relationships and meetings

Go into showbiz
Anna Solakius, Lund

For many years my family hated that I was dancing tango.

My father is from Greece, and in Greece if you say that you're going to dance tango, some people see it to be the same as saying that you're going to become a prostitute. So to my father's ears, it doesn't sound very good. He left Greece in the '60s due to political reasons, and he feels that since we are in this country where we have free education and so many other possibilities, he thinks that it is very strange that I decided to go into showbiz.

I think it took my father ten years before he saw me dancing, and he has never seen me dance live, he only saw it on a video. He said, 'oh, that looks complicated', and then he said, 'what if he drops you', because we were probably doing a lift or something.

'When am I going to be Miss Popular?'
Marija Kaklauskaite, Vilnius

I started wondering, 'hey, when am I going to be invited to do more video shoots?' I've been invited once and they didn't even release the video, it was a commercial for an event at a club. I thought, 'when am I going to be Miss Popular?'

Then I thought that shouldn't be my final goal, but I kept in mind that it would be fun to be in those extra things like video clips. I realised that what I was craving was a team, a crew, to represent, to work hard for. I don't have a crew now.

My older friends who are dancing a lot more than me would like to create a junior team to dance and represent alongside their crew, but I'm not keen on the idea because I don't really like the crew's name they would be called The Junior Uppercuts.

Finnish man
Anni Pilhjarta, Rovaniemi

Even now that I'm a professional dancer, I don't know if my dad has really accepted the idea. He's a really traditional Finnish man, so he thinks that I must have a decent career. He always wanted me to become a doctor or an engineer.

Alexa Wilson, Berlin I mean you can take the girl out of the Pacific, but you can never take the Pacific out of the girl.

An audition
Satoshi Kudo, Stockholm

Back in 2003 I saw a piece that came to Stockholm by Les Ballets C de la B, and the choreography was by Sidi Larbi Cherkaoui. I saw that piece and I was so fascinated, I thought, 'this is good'. There was always this feeling of 'I want to meet this guy'.

In 2006 there was a piece made for Cullberg Ballet by Sidi Larbi, a piece called *End*. I was getting older, I was like 38. I had a friend in the company and I asked this friend, 'could you make arrangements, I would just like to meet him, you know if you go to the bar or something after the show I could meet him, say hello and ask him how he made his piece?'

My friend said, 'he doesn't come to the bar, he doesn't drink, he is still working in the studio after the show'.

She said, 'do you want to come to the studio?'

I was like, 'yeah, sure, I can go to the studio and meet him'.

She said, 'and don't forget to bring your dance clothes'.

I said, 'I am not asking for an audition, I just want to meet him'.

She was like, 'yeah, but just bring them'.

It was like in May that I went to the studio at Cullberg Ballet, and I met Sidi and he asked me, 'so you have material to show me?'

I said, 'Umm, no I don't'.

Later on he told me he thought 'oh, another one, Jesus…'.

So he gave me material, part of the choreography he was making for Cullberg. So I learnt it, it had a lot of arms, and it was not so difficult for me to learn. But he said to me, 'oh, you learn it so fast'.

I was like, 'yeah, we Japanese are very fast at learning'.

He then said, 'okay, do some improvisation', so I did.

I did some movement; I did a little bit of acrobatic stuff. He asked me if I knew any Japanese songs, and I taught him and he recorded it a little bit. We had maybe one and a half hours together and then he said, 'should we go back to town to meet up with the company?'

I was like, 'yeah, let's go back to town'.

As we were walking he said to me, 'so what are you doing this autumn, do you want to join my production?'

I said, 'yeah, yeah, yeah, you don't have to be polite, it is very sweet of you, but a guy like you, you know who you want to work with, you don't need me'.

So I did not take it seriously.

Then that summer I got an email from his producer in Belgium saying 'send us your bank account number', and I was like, 'what do you mean by that? This must be wrong, I have not been hired'.

So they invite me to go in September for a workshop, and they were like 'here is a contract if you'd like to start'. So this is how I began working with Sidi, and it was for a piece called *Myth*.

Working in a factory
Gosia Mielech, Poznań

I felt like I could have stayed in the Polish Dance Theatre forever, it was a family to me in a way. I saw that I had two choices; I could work there from day to day as if I was working in a factory, or I could leave it and experience a totally new life. So I went for the second path, already having in mind the idea of opening DanceLab Company.

I started it with my best friend, who was also my colleague from the Polish Dance Theatre. We had been in ballet school together, so we had known each other for about 15 years. We were not best friends outside of dance, but we were totally best friends when it came to dance. We can understand each other without talking, we have had a mutual respect, similar perceptions of dance, but also we were totally different as dancers – it's like water and fire.

I would just train alone
Marija Kaklauskaite, Vilnius

I met my boyfriend at our dance studio. We've been together for more than one and a half years now. When we were friends I'd always look at him and think, 'he's so good, he must be working hard'. When we started dating, I'd always feel the pressure of failing, doing something wrong or sloppy in my dancing. Before dating him I'd never dance with anyone, I would just train alone. I was not doing so well at events because I'd never give it my all in the studio. I'd rarely talk to him about free styling or events.

As time passed my boyfriend and I would compete together and train together. Right now he's studying and has a hard time coming to the studio. I remind him I still like the way he dances, but that he also has to train daily. We love and enjoy each other's company and dance together with our friends. Sure, we fight sometimes, but our sense of humour and similar hobbies keep us in happiness and harmony.

'I detected the Slavic spirit!'
Iwona Wojnicka, Warsaw

Kylián spoke to me in Polish, because he has Polish heritage. I did a workshop with him, and he seemed shy within this crowd of like 200 people. I saw him alone and I approached him and talked to him, he was so nice.

He asked me, 'where are you from?'

I said 'from Poland'.

He said in Polish, 'I knew it! I detected the Slavic spirit!'

Counting on each other
Uldim Steinam, Riga

In Latvian traditional dance you can't have people missing, there are always eight couples. So it is about being a team. When you dance, you have to count with the other person you are dancing with, you have to be connected, and work strongly as a couple.

You are counting on each other.

It is not about you as an individual. If someone does not know something then everyone must learn it together with that person.

I liked to play football a lot
Rash Sensei, Copenhagen

My big brother taught me how to dance, and he introduced me to breakdance. This is when we lived in the Congo, in the capital, Kinshasa.

I was about 11 years old, and I liked to play football a lot, much more than dancing, but then my brother started to teach me dance and quickly I decided that dancing was my favourite thing to do.

For me, I then worked hard and followed everything that my big brother was saying to me.

Jumping with joy
Maija Rantanen, Espoo

There have been many times when I have almost limped to a dance class, with my knee hurting, or my head aching, thinking, 'am I crazy to go there again?'

But afterwards the pain has gone and I come back from the class almost jumping with joy.

My husband says that dancing makes me a happier person.

A shot of vodka
Magdalena Jankowski, Otrebusy

In our group there's a tradition we have for newcomers after they get their long contract. This tradition means that the newcomer organises a party for everyone in the company. They have to organise the room, the music, drinks and the food.

At the party the company members come and drink a shot of vodka with you. The company members wish you all the best in the group, wishing you good experiences and health. Also, in Polish if you want to be very polite you say to a man 'pan' and to a woman you say 'pani' when talking to them – it is the formal 'you' for males and females, which is kind of like saying 'Mr' and 'Mrs' – but at this party most of the dancers in the company say to the newcomer hosting the party, 'we don't have to call each other 'Mr' or 'Mrs' anymore', things become more informal.

Good for my soul
Marija Kaklauskaite, Vilnius

My dad is a professor and he encourages me to dance, he understands that it is good for me, and good for my health.

But he also knows that it is good for my soul, and that it is healthy to be artistic – some people play instruments, some draw, some sing and I dance.

'90s hip hop
Moa Westerlund, Stockholm

My brother is two years older than me. When I was seven and he was nine, he was into '90s hip hop a lot. I used to imitate the moves he was doing to this music.

One day he took me to his school where there were older guys from the school dancing hip hop. They were dancing much better than me, but I danced there and I got a lot of attention. I was really happy because I was included.

But I remember how easy it was, the rhythm and it was like meeting and playing with others, and finding games within the movement.

His mother chose me
Vita Khlopova, Moscow

My husband is not a dancer, but his mother was my teacher at the Bolshoi Ballet School, and that is how we met. Now we have this joke that he didn't choose me, but his mother chose me!

I had to decide
Susanne Frederiksen, Copenhagen

I had children and I had to decide. I couldn't train, be a dancer, be in performances and also be a mother. So I decided to actually go and just teach, because it fitted more with my family life, I could go and teach in the morning and it works.

Modjgan Hashemian, Berlin I am a political person, I am very interested and active in politics, and that comes from my childhood and family.

Susanne Frederiksen, Copenhagen I realised that dancing was what I wanted to do, but I also wanted to have a family.

The traditional way
Njara Rasolo, Helsinki

Everyone asks me the same question, 'what are you doing here in Helsinki?'

I always say I came here the traditional way; I met a Finnish girl. She was working as a lawyer at the Rwanda Tribunal. We met in Tanzania, and we decided to move to Helsinki.

Living in Finland for me is more than a dream. In Finland I see all the opportunities to help my people in my home country of Madagascar. I am one of the rare dancers from Madagascar who has made it this far, and I have a responsibility for that.

Perfectly round
Özen Erdinc, Malmö

My friend Jessica started a year after me at ballet school, and we became great friends. I was going on 12, and she was going on 11. We met in the dressing room when the new students arrived in autumn.

I remember her as this little girl and she had a problem putting her hair up. Her teacher actually mentioned that her hair was messy, and she needed to fix it. Her hair looked like it had exploded, and she couldn't fix it herself, so I took care of it. I helped her put her hair in a bun, and that became a routine. She would sit on her knees, and I sat on a bench, and I did her ponytail and put her hair in a perfectly round bun.

That's it
Piotr Zalipski, Otrebusy

I met my wife at the dance group. I remember my friends and I were sitting in the ballet class watching the new dancers.

My friend from the choir asked me, 'and what do you think about her?' I was like, 'I think she will be my wife'. That was it.

A complete mess
Oxana Bellamy, Helsinki

I was passing by a dance studio and I heard a magnificent sound, it was drums. I thought, 'I want to dance to that sound! I must dance to it!'

This was Afro dance.

I went to the first lesson, but I was so scared the whole time because I was a complete mess. I remember afterwards the teacher found me in the corridor. I had my back to him and he tapped me on my shoulder, and I turned around.

He said, 'you know you are doing very well, you have to carry on'.

If he had never told me that I never would have carried on. After that I felt more confident, and I think he probably realised that I needed that boost.

Hang people's coats
Niina Vahtola, Oulu

When I was with the folk dance group people were always doing things together, they were like a community. I had been dancing in dance studios for a million years, and I never had that kind of friendship, it was not like a community.

I remember with the folk dance group, when we were going to foreign countries to perform we had to try to get money to help support our travels.

Sometimes we would stand in a restaurant lobby, and we would hang people's coats for money. I just loved doing it because we were doing it together.

When I compared that to my ballet years, I thought to myself, 'what on earth have I been doing, why didn't I come to a group like this earlier?'

Finland and Russia
Oxana Bellamy, Helsinki

I am Russian, and I was born in St Petersburg. I notice that my dancing friends at the dance school who are Finnish greet me in a friendly way. This is not necessarily normal because the history between Finland and Russia has been difficult at times.

But when you have a common hobby like dance, and you are dancing together, it changes people. It is no longer so much about old politics, it is about people being nice and understanding. It is all community, and I think it is a nice thing.

'Does anyone like to dance here?'
Jo Parkes, Berlin

In the context that I am working in now, with refugees, I cannot go into the workshops I facilitate with a man, so I have a female film team I work with. The dancers involved are dancers I know. Also I try to find artists who are new to the region, or dancers who are refugees themselves, and integrate them into the team. We now have two artists who are on the programme who came to Germany themselves as refugees, and one who has lived in an accommodation centre, so they know the system.

There is a lot of putting posters up and making calls for people to join the teaching team, but then there is also just a lot of asking. I spend a lot of time hanging around corridors and saying, 'oh, does anyone like playing music here? Does anyone like to dance here?'

How romantic
Anna Solakius, Lund

My tango teacher and I got together, now we are dance partners and romantic partners. It can be challenging, but we have known each other for 15 years.

132 *Dance, Diversity and Difference*

Krysztof Fijak, Otrebusy My daughters don't like to dance, they prefer sports like track and field.

When you are quite young, you go through a lot of different stages. In the beginning, we of course had a stage of falling in love, being super romantic, and dancing tango on top of that, how romantic can that be! I mean that's like the biggest dream. Going from that, there's a realisation that he's more advanced in tango than me, and I was still feeling like his student. I think I've gone through quite severe jealousy and asking myself why am I getting jealous and for what?

Being partners in life and partners in dance, you are always together. We fight a lot, not in class, but around teaching, just because of how our dynamics are. Both of us are very energetic and outgoing, so we have found that collaboration is not always easy. This has been something that we've been trying to work on – how we can collaborate better.

Win the competition
Niina Vahtola, Oulu

In the ballet class, the girls I danced with weren't friends, I felt like we were just training together. I think there was always a competition going on among us, and I felt like I was never the one to win the competition. I think I was too young to understand a lot of the dynamics going on, and to understand why I was not the one getting the solos.

Student concerts
Vadim Kasparov, St Petersburg

I moved from Baku to St Petersburg to study at the University of Physical Education. It was in the Soviet Union time, I was 18 years old, and at that point my background was in sports, I had nothing to do with dance.

At university in St Petersburg I organised some student concerts. It was at these concerts that I met my wife, Natalia. Natalia's background was in artistic gymnastics, and she made some very good choreography with the students for the student concerts.

Over time, as we did more student events we found that we had a student dance group. Natalia continued to make the dance works and dealt with the artistic things, and I tried to find places that they could perform. We are a good team.

He was over 100 years old
Vita Khlopova, Moscow

Igor Moiseyev was still alive when I was dancing with Moiseyev Dance Company. He was over 100 years old, and he was still there in the theatre with us.

For us dancers, if he was in the rehearsal or on the stage it was like we would work harder than any other time, he inspired us.

Unique for me
Oxana Bellamy, Helsinki

Partner dancing is very interesting to me.

I have noticed that sometimes you cannot speak the same verbal language as your dancing partner, but with body language you can speak and understand each other. When a partner dances well, you do not need to even speak.

I think you do not need to speak to dance very well.

This dance family
Eveniya Kim, St Petersburg

The dance company is our family, and it is our whole life now. When we are not working we are thinking about it. Vitaly and I are married to it, literally! It is who we are.

Here in St Petersburg people like ballet, everyone knows about ballet, and contemporary dance, okay, a few people know about this, but then experimental performance, people say 'what?' So as we do this work we have to remember that we are working in a small area and this dance family we have created is very small in comparison to the city, and the rest of the country.

'So underground'
Veera Lamberg, Helsinki

Sometimes you get so blind when you are immersed in the dance world.

I am lucky to have a little sister who is interested in dance, but she is not in professional dance circles. She has been saying to me 'contemporary dance is so underground still'.

I have said, 'I think it is better now, people know what contemporary dance is', but my sister is like 'I'm not sure…'.

Dance is amazing for body awareness, so I think it should be for everybody, and because I am so 'in' it I think it is everywhere. But perhaps that is not the case.

Making a small dance group
Uldim Steinam, Riga

I started dancing when I was 15 years old, mostly because of my mother. There was the *Song and Dance Celebration*, and she was making a small dance group. Because I was her son I had to join.

It was in 1950, and since then I have attended all the *Song and Dance Celebration* events, every five years.

I've never been a professional dancer, it is not my education, some people learn choreography and performing, but I studied to be an electrical engineer. But my mother got me into it, and I joined the dancing community, and before I knew it I was leading this folk dance group.

Everyone in my family dances, they are like me, not professional but they dance.

My hero
Laura Lohi, Malmö

There is one guy I work with who is really like my hero. He has had Parkinson's disease for about 30 years. He seems to have a lot of different kinds of days, so he never seems to be the same when he comes to the class. At first when I met him, I thought he looked very stiff, he doesn't have dyskinesia but he can't suddenly do anything.

Laura Lohi, Malmö I have never been into making pieces, so I thought community work could be for me.

A good example of this wasn't in a dance class, but it was before one of the classes. It had been snowing a lot and everything was white and bright, and he was coming in through the door with his wife. I greeted him and held the door open for him. He was just stood there, he couldn't move. He had closed his eyes, and his wife explained that this was how he is with Parkinson's; the light was too bright and he can't see and he can't move.

So he was just standing there, making these tiny steps, but he didn't move forward. I was in shock and thinking, 'what happened?'

His wife told him to take a deep breath. I felt really bad because I was holding the door for him, I think he heard my voice, and he probably knew that I was holding the door, and maybe got a little stressed that he had to come in because everyone was waiting for him. So I started chatting to his wife, and so on, then she told him to take a deep breath, and counted '1, 2, 3' before he took a step. He suddenly opened his eyes and he walked, like nothing had happened.

That was the moment that I realised that this is how it is, you see the people coming here to take class, and they have made the effort; it is probably a good day for them because they are here. One of the most beautiful parts of the class is seeing the relationships with their partners, the person they came with; there's so much love. When they look at each other and when they smile at each other, and they dance together; we have this thing at the end of the class, where everyone is in a circle holding hands, and we give a little squeeze of the hands of the person next to you, and we look at the person in the eye, to thank them. I almost cry at that moment because they are usually standing with their partners or relatives, and there is this beautiful connection.

A medicine
Santa Claus, Rovaniemi

When I meet children, we always dance around. We take hands and dance in a circle. It's fantastic. The children's joy is my reward. It is a medicine, if I have anything wrong in my life. When I see the children's joy, that is amazing to me.

When I see people dancing, adults too, it is the same joy. I can see how they enjoy it.

Dance is the same all around the world. The steps are a bit different, but the feeling is the same.

7
Heritage and history

The day that the Wall came down
Volker Eisenach, Berlin

The opening night of my first big performance was the day after the Berlin Wall came down. The group I was dancing with knew this date would be our opening night about a year earlier; we'd made the decision to open the show at the beginning of November. Bad timing.

I remember I had a dress rehearsal the day that the Wall came down. The next morning I was at home with my mum and she was reading the newspaper. I saw the cover of the newspaper and I said, 'what is that stupid picture of all the German flags and people standing on the Wall?'

Because that just didn't happen, I mean no one would stand on the Wall and you didn't see many German flags around and you'd never see people waving flags in the streets.

I thought, 'is it an advertisement?'
My mum said, 'it's the Wall'.
I said, 'what Wall?'
She was like, '*the* Wall'.
I replied, 'WHAT? What happened?'
She said, 'it's open'.
I was in shock. I said, 'wait a minute, it's open?'
So I missed the opening of the Berlin Wall because I was in the dress rehearsal for my first big performance.

Ordinary clothes
Maija Rantanen, Espoo

There are certain Finnish dance phenomena that I clearly remember from early in my life called the *Saturday Dance Nights*. This was a very popular TV show in the '70s and '80s.

Thinking about it now it was quite a strange thing to watch, because it was just a group of ordinary people who danced in a studio as if they were in a Saturday night dance hall. An orchestra played tangos, waltzes and foxtrots and people danced in a solemn and serious way, in their ordinary clothes.

Actually it was not so much like watching a TV show, but more like watching a fire burning in a fireplace. To watch this show, after Saturday night's sauna, was a favourite pastime for my family.

Badge of honour
Alexa Wilson, Berlin

You wouldn't think here, in the middle of Europe, you'd get a curator walking out of a performance art festival because they are finding a performance all too much. I've had that happen and I feel like I can wear a badge of honour that I am challenging people in that way.

Doing what I do, I realise that I might get push back, and that people might say some harsh things. I mean it is not that you are trying to create division, but work that is controversial does do that, and it does create polarisation.

I get the feeling that Europe doesn't want to create division because of its history and it has seen what division does, but ironically this is now what is happening in Europe anyway!

Safe on the stage
Hanna Raszewska, Warsaw

The first time that I went to Greece I was shocked that they have folk dance happening in lots of communities. We don't have that here in Poland, we have our folk dances on a stage.

The Union of Soviet Socialist Republics seemed to think that folk dance was safe on the stage, and that it was a way to construct a national identity and unify all nations in this part of Europe.

There was World War I, World War II, and then after that there was the hard time for our dances in Poland to survive in local communities.

Pass it on
Anamet Magven, Læsø

To be able to come back to my culture, to the place where I grew up, it feels like it makes sense to go back to my hometown and pass on what I have experienced and learnt while being abroad and in other cities.

I think there is openness in this small place, there are new reforms in schools, and there is an opening for dance to make an entrance. I am quite excited about it all.

Bag with the wheels
Marija Kaklauskaite, Vilnius

Sometimes at competitions you see older people competing. They might not be doing all the moves anymore, but they are still there and getting involved.

I think the behaviour of older people competing in hip hop and street dance is similar to how my grandparents behave. My grandmother still tells us that she wants to cook dinner, and my grandfather never listens to my mother when she tells him to take the bag with the wheels to carry things from the supermarket. They are older than us and they want their independence, they want to be out there and to keep pushing what they can do.

It is the same with the dancing; I think you don't want to stop just because you get older.

Putting blinkers over your eyes
Gosia Mielech, Poznań

It's important to remember that there are many wonderful Polish teachers and choreographers. I mean there are nationalists who think the Polish way of moving is good enough, and would say 'what is the point of bringing in these foreign ways of moving?'

Honestly, for me questions such as this are just stupidity, it is putting blinkers over your eyes to ignore what is going on in the rest of the world. You can't lose anything in being open to other stimuli, and other people.

I think there will be a tendency in Poland for people to close themselves off, because for the last few years we have been really open and embracing all of this. For me, it has been a good time to be based in Poland, it is very easy to travel and perform abroad. However, taking under consideration the government that is in Poland right now, and what is happening in Europe we will close ourselves again, there will not be so much freedom and curiosity in dance and that really worries me.

Louise or Jessica
Özen Erdinc, Malmö

At ballet school I was the only student who came from the ghetto, and the other students were usually from finer Swedish families. I think I was the only foreigner, and I was definitely the only Turkish girl there.

I had a name that was very difficult to pronounce, so of course others noticed I was different. It was not that I was different from the way I spoke or dressed, but I was different because of my name. It was like, 'yes, I'm Turkish', because I wasn't called Louise or Jessica, or another common name.

Closer to the ground
Edmundus Zicka, Vilnius

From what I can see, stage dancing in Lithuania is trying to keep as close to the authentic traditional dancing roots as possible, it is not going too classical. Each step has its own name, and this has been written down. In relation to the leg positions, the arm positions, and the movement, people are trying to keep it closer to the ground of what the folk dance has been.

Only five pictures
Iwona Wojnicka, Warsaw

In Berlin I went to an archive and I saw pictures of one of Mary Wigman's performances, and it was during the time when there was a Polish dancer in her group.

In the archive I drew sketches of these pictures. So I started with these images as my beginning point for making choreography and I made a solo. There were only five pictures to work from, but they provided a great source of inspiration.

Creating community
Uldim Steinam, Riga

I am 80 years old, I have seen the history of Latvia over time and how dance has been part of this history. During Soviet times there were certain ideological things connected to dancing that were being pushed by one side or the other. There have been certain events where dance has provided a foundation for identity to be held onto and exerted.

In my opinion the *Song and Dance Festival* has contributed to the relationships the Baltic States have with each other today. It has brought the countries together, it has helped find national identities, and I think it has helped us avoid situations like what has happened in the Ukraine.

I think there is not war here in Latvia because we work together to keep our culture, to keep traditions and find an identity that is collective. I think dance events are actually a very big and powerful thing for creating community. From what I witnessed dance is something that helped us gain independence from the Soviet Union.

Uldim Steinam, Riga I never started dancing with the intention of making a big statement.

Laughing at the dinner table
Maija Rantanen, Espoo

I think of dancing in connection with the heavy burden of the Finnish Lutheran tradition I've experienced. Here, in the dark and cold northern part of the world, I think people can be sullen and solitary. In my family dancing has been seen as a frivolity, and to my religious mother it is even seen as a sin! There has been a constant feeling of shame, not being allowed to laugh at the dinner table, and not being encouraged to express oneself.

So from this upbringing, to finding myself in a dance class where Cuban teachers flaunt their smile and dig out that hidden sensuality, it is quite the opposite of extremes for me. Comments from the teachers like, 'mujeres, your hips! Shake 'em! Chest up, flirt with me!' are hard for a 56 year old like me, but it is so much fun, so who cares!

Maybe we Finns are a great dancing nation despite the Lutheran burden of laughing at the dinner table being considered a sin, and despite our aversion to close contact with other people. Maybe the melancholy heard in the Finnish tango is a clue here – the attraction of opposites. One of our most popular tangos is *Satumaa*, which translates as 'the fairytale land'. In this song the singer dreams of going far away to a sunny land where the sun shines and everyone is happy. Sunny land far away, smiling people – send a couple of Cubans here to Finland and 'bang!' – two opposites meet.

At home it was always Polish
Magdalena Jankowski, Otrebusy

I'm the only German dancer in the dance group. Most of the other dancers and singers are Polish. We sing in Polish, so even if you are not Polish you have to know the Polish language.

My parents did a good job speaking with me in Polish at home, there was no German at home, and I was not allowed to speak German. German was for outside, German was for in kindergarten and in school, but at home it was always Polish.

There are also foreigners in the group, from the Ukraine or Belarus. There is one man from Brazil and another from Belgium, they don't have any Polish roots but they learnt the language because they were fascinated by the art of folk dance.

Magdalena Zalipska, Otrebusy I like dancing the Kujawiak dance, it is full of contrasts, on one hand it is very lyrical and romantic, and on the other hand it is very dynamic and lively.

Fast culture
Eveniya Kim, St Petersburg

I think the problem of developing contemporary dance here in Russia is deep-rooted. I think the challenge of allowing new contemporary forms of dance to flourish here is to do with the culture of our country and how this has evolved. Culture nowadays is focused on either high culture, for example the ballet, the theatre, the Bolshoi, and patriotic culture, or alternatively it is focused on fast culture, for example dance on TV. Neither of these cultures are focused on contemporary art, and there is no apparent or obvious place for contemporary art and dance in these spaces.

I am not a pineapple
Modjgan Hashemian, Berlin

I don't like the word 'roots', but my identity as an Iranian-German, or whatever you want to call me, has played a big role in my work.

When I say I am German people are like, 'yeah, well … no, really where are you from?'

I reply, 'to be honest I was born in Berlin, I have a German passport, I have grown up here a lot, what more do you want?'

This labelling of people is so boring and so tiring. This is something that is to do with my work now, where I am actively fighting against labelling people, and against using and abusing people because of their nationalities. People always say to me 'this is so exotic' when looking at the work I do, and I am like, 'no, I am not a pineapple, I am not a mango, so don't call me exotic please'.

Of course cultures and places leave some things in your identity, and I think that has something to do with how you are brought up, your parents, what is valued and important. I mean when I hear Iranian music something happens inside of me, but still I don't think it is important to label or frame this as a nationality. It is a feeling that you have.

Dancing every day
Njara Rasolo, Helsinki

I come from Madagascar. It is maybe one of the poorest countries in the world, but actually there is a lot of dancing happening there. As a culture, there is dancing almost every day, in all kinds of traditions and situations.

In the city where I grew up everyone had a dance group. If you didn't have a dance group there was something wrong with you, and you would never get respect, and you would never attract a girl or anything!

Can leave a kind of wound
Jo Parkes, Berlin

I went this week to Dresden for my first meeting about a new dance project in the city. In Dresden the Pegida movement is strong; it is where the biggest marches happen every Monday.

The current dynamic in Dresden is very interesting. You have a generation there who grew up in war, and they are very old now, and then many other people grew up in East Germany, the DDR. Those who grew up in the DDR experienced very similar things to what the refugees we see now coming into Germany are going through, but without moving. They stayed in the same place but their whole system changed. That must do something to you.

I am interested in researching the theme of tradition in this context. The issues of diversity and multiculturalism are so problematic in Dresden, and the history of Germany is so raw there. It is not that I want to convey any sense of right wing fundamentalism in any way, but I do get that if your world is forcibly changed in any way that can leave a kind of wound in you and makes you respond in certain ways.

The anarchy commune
Anastasia Patsey, St Petersburg

I feel that the location of 10 Pushkinskaya is deeply rooted in the St Petersburg cultural landscape. It started in 1989, and it started as a squat.

So if you go back to the situation of culture and arts in the Soviet times it was very ideologically based and controlled throughout the whole twentieth century. Then in the 1980s there was a jump in terms of arts in Russia becoming more liberal. But that said, throughout the whole repression period of culture there were still artists who worked outside of the 'normal' framework, and who didn't want to be members of official unions that were organised, they often worked in an underground situation. There were many words to determine this culture, some say 'underground' or 'Leningrad underground', some say 'nonconformist art' or 'second culture', others say 'unofficial culture' – many words are used to talk about the same thing, but here at 10 Pushkinskaya we use the word 'nonconformist'.

At the end of the '80s the nonconformist movement was very strong, and paradoxically already institutionalised because these nonconformist artists already had a union. The artists squatted in this house at 10 Pushkinskaya, and it was supposed to be renovated. The whole building had around 300 flats, so it was very big, around 4,500 square metres. It was one of the biggest squats at that time in Leningrad; it was not the only one, but perhaps the liveliest. Around this time the artists squatting here had this choice of either taking an anarchist strategy, like other artists say in Berlin did, or to choose to formalise themselves, and this is what they did. So they had an agreement made with the city, that the city, with support of investors, would renovate the building, because it was half ruined and was not safe for anyone to be here. The building was renovated and then it was divided up. Two-thirds of the building went back to the city as payment for the renovation, and the artists received the rest of the building.

From the 1990s the anarchy commune of 10 Pushkinskaya started to transform, which is a very interesting process because now we have this very mixed identity. We still try to sustain this anarchy feeling, for example, in the way our yard looks, because people come here to also have this nostalgia feeling about the 'good old days'. Then we have the museum component, and we have a collection and it is a museum in a more traditional sense. Then another component it is still a commune, because we have 40 artists who live and work here in the house, they have their studios here, which for many of them are also living spaces, and some of them live in these spaces with their families. Then there are three other studios that belong to the St Petersburg Art Residency and so we have this international component.

So all of this exists under one roof. The activities therefore are very different, because there are visual artists, musicians and performers together in the space, and then we also have an educational programme that also includes diverse projects. It is wide reaching.

Two airports and two zoos
Volker Eisenach, Berlin

In Berlin there is now one big ballet company – we used to have three companies, two in the East and one in the West. When the Berlin Wall came down there was not the money to continue them all, so now we have one.

The problem was not just with dance companies; Berlin had two of everything, two airports and two zoos. When we became one country everything got merged, and there was struggle and fighting in the merging. But in my view it was the best possible thing to do.

Lots of buttons
Raivis Dzjamko, Riga

The company I started to dance with was a folk dance group, but they had started to do more modern things. We did not just dance in straight lines and

Volker Eisenach, Berlin Sometimes there is not enough money for the arts due to the history of the two Berlins, East and West. When the unification came the money stopped coming in but Berlin kept spending.

circles, but there was something freer about the dances we performed. There were pieces just for guys, with lots of cartwheels and tricks.

In Latvian folk dance there are always very elaborate costumes, with many layers, complicated fastenings and lots of buttons. The director of the company took off some of these layers and made the costumes less complicated. I know that there were people who kept saying, 'why are you ruining our traditional costumes?'

But I think we need to remember that these costumes are from many years ago, we do not wear clothes like this anymore in day-to-day life, so why should we preserve them on stage? It's like in the morning when you go to wash your face you are not wearing your full Latvian dance costume!

Katerina Urbanovich, St Petersburg I don't think we should ever say, 'no, we don't dance Western contemporary dance', I think it is important to explore everything, but not to copy.

Every big factory
Vadim Kasparov, St Petersburg

My wife, Natalia, and I called our school Dance House because it is like a home. We want it to feel like family, but at the same time we don't want to close people out and make them feel like they can't be in the family, we are open. I think this was a smart way to do it because of our history here in Russia.

In the Soviet times most people were involved in the arts. In this district of St Petersburg alone there were five different houses of culture, and almost every big factory had their own house of culture. This is where the workers would go to see the theatre, dance or ballet, and where they could also be involved in music ensembles, ballet for adults and theatre groups. This was very normal, and people were totally involved in the arts – not just in relation to education, but also in relation to life. In Soviet times there was care about the cultural development of people, this is why we have so many theatres and the ballet, because the people were not just spectators who wanted to be entertained for fun, people really understood the different aspects of the different art forms. It was the government policy.

When the Soviet Union collapsed all of these houses of culture were closed, some of them were destroyed, and some of them were turned into business centres or offices. For many people who had been involved in culture, there was now nothing for them to do, nowhere for them to take classes or be involved in arts groups.

So when we started our dance school we wanted to focus on those people who really miss the arts, adults who want to develop their artistic expression and have a place to go to be in an artistic community.

Too commercial
Njara Rasolo, Helsinki

I mainly work with street dance styles, but behind that is the philosophy of hip hop and the history that comes with that. I use my hip hop background as a tool, with the same philosophy as it had in its past – to make the world better. So for me, I don't want the street dance I do to be too commercial, I like to keep it connected to where it has come from, the hip hop roots.

8

Change and turning points

47 minutes
Uldim Steinam, Riga

It was 23 August 1988. Latvia was still under Soviet control, but this was starting to fall and change was in the air.

There was a rock opera at a big stadium here in Riga. Many people participated in this rock opera, and the producer asked me to make the dances. I was told 'it will just be a few dances, something small, nothing major, nothing special'. I then found out that all the best Latvian musicians would be performing there, the ballet soloists were dancing, everyone was volunteering to be part of the event. I worked with about 100 dancers, and there was a risk that we could be taken to prison at any moment, because it was considered to be an anti-Soviet event. We didn't even know if the concert would start because there was a demonstration and aggressive people outside the stadium.

We stood on the stage for 47 minutes waiting to start, the audience were clapping, there were tears in their eyes, they brought flowers to the concert. For 47 minutes they did not stop clapping. The stadium was full, there was no free space. Even the most well known people in Latvia attended and just sat on the ground or stood with everyone else.

Over time I have seen many performances and many different audiences, but I have never ever seen anything like this. I was brought to that moment by dancing. While standing on stage there was the most incredible feeling of a deep connection to this very significant moment in history.

'You don't ride on camels?!'
Modjgan Hashemian, Berlin

I think part of what I do is educate people through my dance works, to avoid the continuing questions like, 'you don't ride on camels?!' When I was in Tel Aviv I really got this question a lot. I had a dinner where I invited a lot of dancers and choreographers, we were sitting there and I was introducing them to the dance scene in Iran and they were like 'wow, amazing, we didn't know that people there lived like us!' But then I think there is really a need for us to do this, to talk about it, show what is happening.

I think one of the nice effects of this movement and change in the world is that we can see and experience difference more. It is so nice to go through the streets here in Kreuzberg and listen to different languages, and through experiencing this difference I think people are learning from each other and getting to know each other's music and food. I think this is the best thing that could have happened, this movement of people, and these conversations of 'well, I will show you how it is from my perspective'.

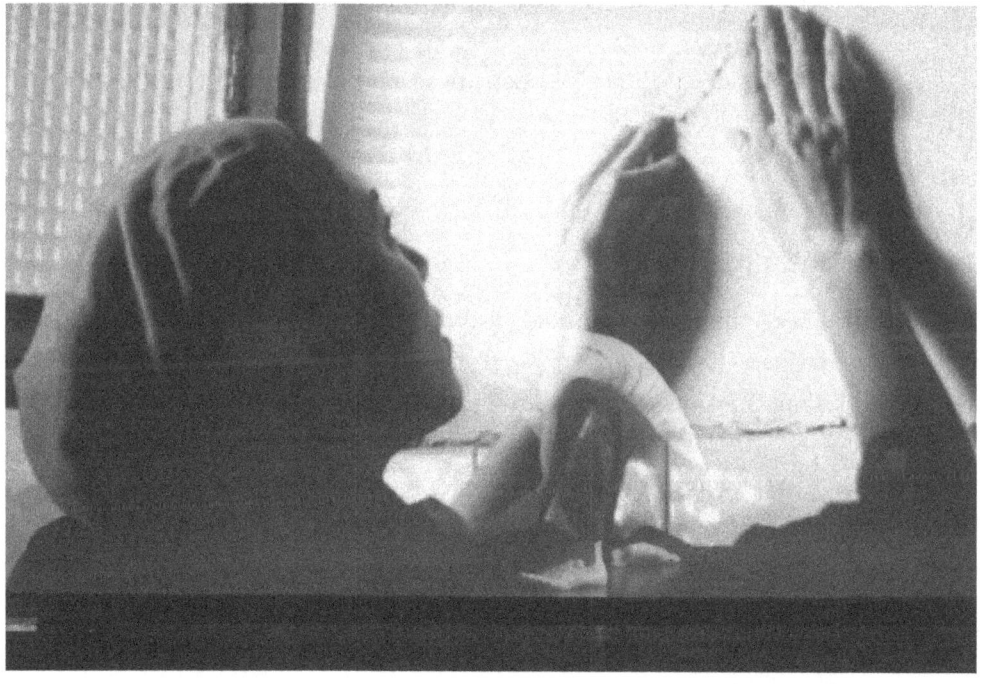

Modjgan Hashemian, Berlin I am quite focused on women in my dance work, not because I want to say 'women are better', but because I think because women come up short in many discussions.

Edmundus Zicka, Vilnius Now dancing is more like a hobby for me, it is more for my soul.

My turnout
Anni Pilhjarta, Rovaniemi

By the time I was about 15 years old, I started to realise that maybe I'm not really suited to be a ballet dancer. My turnout wasn't good enough, my hips and my ankles are not good. I was so determined about the training, but I knew the reality of the ballet world. I found out about the dance programme at the Tampere Conservatory, and I thought, 'oh wow, there's a school for folk dance'. I thought that might be the place for me.

Hide away and watch television
Alexa Wilson, Berlin

I arrived in Berlin during the financial crisis of 2008, so my entire time in Berlin has been during a very unstable period in Europe. Because things are changing so fast and things are unstable, I actually feel it is a really exciting time to make art right now on the planet, to hide away and watch television to me is just exacerbating the problems that have caused the instability.

For me the really good side to this vulnerability the world is experiencing is that it's connected to intimacy, and it can draw people closer together. Something that really interests me is being able to harness the positive, and the connection and the intimacy, and being moved and moving each other through this vulnerability.

Bam!
Satoshi Kudo, Stockholm

In 1990, Mats Ek's *Giselle* by Cullberg Ballet came to Tokyo. Of course I knew nothing about the Swedish dance scene at that time. I was not even paying attention.

One of my teachers said to me, 'Satoshi, you must go and see this show, they are from Sweden and they are doing something very interesting'. The tickets were not selling because they were completely unknown in Japan, so I got a free ticket. I went along and it was like, 'Bam! *Giselle* by Mats Ek'.

I literally cried, and after the show I did not feel like I had seen a dance performance. You know sometimes when you see a dance performance and you think, 'wow, that was a nice dance performance, with nice music and nice technique'. No, it was not like that at all I was purely touched by the story, which was a very new experience for me and nothing like any other dance performance I had ever seen. I got totally hooked.

A year later Cullberg Ballet came back to do *Giselle* again and then *Swan Lake*. I saw the shows a couple of times and I was fascinated. I think I must have been 21 or 22 years old, and I just had no idea about how to associate myself with it, with the size of the company, or the level, and my ballet technique was obviously not at all good enough, far from it.

But at that age, in Tokyo, working in show business, I would say that I had confidence, and at the time I was like, 'Yeah, maybe I will try'. It was nice because I didn't know what to be afraid of.

Real ballet life inside out
Gosia Mielech, Poznań

While studying at ballet school, I was also an apprentice in the Opera House in Poznań. Thanks to this experience, I realised that ballet was not going to be my future. I had a chance to taste the real ballet life inside out, and I knew this road wouldn't be the right one for me. With all due respect, it is such devoted work and yet you get so little fulfilment from it. In my opinion it is hard to be an individual in ballet, you just interpret the work, follow and fit an ideal.

While studying in ballet school we had contemporary classes as well, I fell in love with that kind of movement. After graduating I was lucky enough to get a job in the Polish Dance Theatre. It all happened very quickly, so I didn't need to audition anywhere else.

Washing glasses in a bar
Hanna Raszewska, Warsaw

During the day I would be a professor teaching dance at the University, and I would be like, 'welcome students, today we are talking about Doris Humphrey'. Then at night I was washing glasses in a bar or waiting tables in a restaurant. It was hard.

I then decided to quit working jobs that were not connected to my dance profession, but it's really hard to live from being a freelancer dance theoretician if you don't have another job simultaneously.

Guillermo the Wonder Boy
Maija Rantanen, Espoo

I danced salsa classes taught by a Finnish woman for two years. Then she left for maternity leave, and then my life changed – although I didn't know it then.

Suddenly one day there was a young Cuban boy standing as the teacher at the front of the class. I was horrified. He was Cuban, so he could see immediately how badly I danced. He was a young man, and I thought, 'I can never look at his butt!'

But as I discovered, butts have to be looked at, if you want to learn. This young guy, Guillermo Zayas, was a wonder boy. He did not speak English; he did not speak to us middle-aged clumsy ladies in those morning classes at all. But still he succeeded in teaching us complex choreographies and sowed the love for all different types of Cuban music – salsa, son, mambo, rumba.

It was like Guillermo the Wonder Boy didn't see our mistakes. He never pointed out our shortcomings. We did lots of repetition in a friendly atmosphere, and the trance-like attraction of Cuban rhythms helped me stay focused. Maybe the Cuban 'mañana' attitude was also helping here, the idea that you don't have to be perfect now, straight away, in this class. Step by step, keep practising and then, maybe, you'll learn.

A moment to just be
Jo Parkes, Berlin

I don't want to paint what is happening to those who are refugees in a positive light. Whether it is about economics, or if it is about plight, nobody puts their kids in a boat that might sink for no reason. Nobody. But within this entire trauma, there have been two beautiful things that have emerged for me.

At the last dance party we had at the refugee accommodation centre, as everyone was leaving there were four men left. I was cleaning up with the DJ, putting the chairs away, and these four men were helping. The music was still on and then the four men were just dancing. It was really clear, on a very subtle level, that they were gay, the four of them, and that when everyone had gone they had a moment to just be who they were – which I imagine is impossible in an accommodation centre, because there is just no private space. I think that is the kind of nice thing about setting up something in the arts world where there is the opportunity to set up these spaces, people have a different opportunity to be who they are.

The other story is of an extraordinary friend of mine, who was a teacher in Syria, and she is about the same age as me – so in her early 40s. She was considered too old to get married; she just missed the window to find a man. But on her flight here to Germany she met a lovely man from the other side of Syria, who she would never normally meet and probably would normally never be allowed to marry. He is a little bit younger than her, they fell in love, got married and she has just had a baby. For her there is a whole new life that she thought she never would have. I think that is really exciting in terms of being a woman, there is something extraordinarily difficult, but also extraordinarily empowering when you are in this situation where your role shifts.

I mean I don't want to polarise the different cultures, but if you are a woman – and this is the huge challenge of my work – to be there as a woman, to be seen as a woman through a context that does not agree with me sometimes is a challenge. I have never felt more like a woman, I never really considered my gender or reflected on it. In this context of working with refugees I am really aware of being a woman. This is also why we have an all-female team, and when we do the dance parties it is all women – just to offer role models. The spaces that we make for interactions through dance are quite prescribed; the gender roles are very visible and very public. You know at the dance parties, there is a row of women not dancing. I mean I can dabke with the best of them – I can do Lebanese or Palestinian – but it is not often I am dancing with the men, and of course not, because it is not necessarily culturally acceptable.

But then there is the whole thing going on for me, because where I am coming from it is culturally acceptable for males and females to dance together. I think, 'I better go and sit with the women', but then I think, 'I have to dance'. There is this whole internal narrative that goes on for me that is very complex when I join a group of people dancing on the dance floor. This all involves huge questions about cultural identity, and the questions are very visible in the moment when you choose to take someone's hand and dance with them.

'Okay, shit! It is time!'
Özen Erdinc, Malmö

I will never forget the audition I did for the Finnish National Ballet. I struggled throughout the two years I was at the Royal Swedish Ballet School with the concept of fouetté pirouettes. I always thought, 'how on earth do you do this?' Was it my stamina? Was it my strength in my leg? I couldn't figure it out.

I learnt to do neat clean ones compared to my classmates; I think I got to even 16, and it was my final year where I should be able to handle 32 fouettés on pointe. My teacher said that I should be able to do it, as it would definitely be in auditions, and the auditions were starting in the autumn.

I mean fouettés are essentially just up and down while turning, and it should not be a big deal. I didn't know what was wrong with me and why I couldn't do them, so I feared the idea of having to do fouettés in an audition.

I remembered that the audition for the Finnish National Ballet was going really well. But when we came to the fouettés, I was like, 'oh my God!' because I was convinced that my flaws would be revealed. I tried to wait for the last group, hoping that they would forget me. I ended up having to go with a girl from my class at the Royal Swedish Ballet School, she was a tall girl called Johanna, who could just spin, and do 64 fouettés with hands on the hips, doubles and triples.

The jury said, 'okay the last group, please take your places, two girls doing fouettés'.

I was like, 'okay, shit! It is time!', and we started doing fouettés.

We started and Johanna dropped out. I don't know what happened, I don't remember if she picked up the fouettés again but I found myself continuing without her. The first 32 fouettés of my life happened during that audition, and I ended up finishing just in front of the director and the ballet master – I almost ended up in their laps because I travelled so much from the back of the room. I ended up just in front of them with this huge smile and walked away really cool, pretending that it was the sort of thing I did everyday.

All my classmates in the audition were shocked because they had never seen me do anything like that before. They came up to me saying, 'what the hell did you do?', but I just said casually, 'I don't know'.

That's how I got into the Finnish National Ballet.

Not going to take me down
Veera Lamberg, Helsinki

When I was a teenager I realised that I had to put some more energy into dancing in order to really have a chance to be a professional. I tried to get into some sort of class for the more talented dancers. I got into one of these classes, and I was in high school.

But I really don't have the ideal dancer's body, so that was a struggle for me and I was not able to take part in the National Ballet School training and things like that. But somehow I just decided that was not going to take me down, I still enjoyed ballet, and I enjoy it even now, and that is important for me.

I just had to realise that this is my body and I do what I can with it. Surprisingly you can do quite a few things when you start to work with your body.

'Why not?'
Moa Westerlund, Stockholm

I found some joy in dancing hip hop, and I started doing jazz for one year when I was nine years old. Then my teacher, Kristina, said to me, 'maybe you should apply for this ballet school'. I didn't know anything about ballet, but I thought 'why not?'

Piotr Zalipski, Otrębusy The Nowy Sącz is a dance just for boys. As the soloist I had to do a movement like a butterfly jumping, not using your hands on the floor at all, seven times around the stage. That is hard.

Award after award
Volker Eisenach, Berlin

Royston Muldoom contacted me when he came back to Berlin and was working the Berliner Philharmoniker. He said he was looking for an assistant and asked if I would be interested in the role. That's how I started working with Berlin Philharmonic on these huge productions with 250 dancers.

The first dance production was *Sacre du Printemps*, which was documented in the film *Rhythm is it*. Everyone thought *Rhythm is it* was going to be a little art house film, everyone including the producers thought it would be seen in some festivals maybe a few schools, but that is it. Then it took off, and it won award after award.

I think it changed the dance world in Germany quite a lot, and showed people sitting at the desks deciding what money to give to dance, what dance was capable of. I think it illustrated that dance can reach out into communities and it is not only stuff you do at school for the little Christmas show.

Then there was the chimney!
Cher Geurtze, Copenhagen

I had to find a new location for Uppercut Dance Company and the community dance project called *Dans in Nordvest*. I needed a dance space that was big enough to accommodate our growing needs. I began to look at some churches that the city was going to close down. Then I got an email on a Friday afternoon that said, 'the crematorium at the top of the hill at Bispebjerg has closed down'.

I went to look at it and the whole place was locked up, there were signs saying: 'don't go inside'. I went all the way around the back, thinking how do I get into this place? I saw the round chapel space and I could figure out that wouldn't be big enough for a studio, and from the back side of the building everything was dug down into the ground, like cellar rooms and there were no windows. I thought 'oh no', and then there was the chimney!

But I thought 'okay, I'm here now, I should look'.

I got the telephone number that was written on the door and I called it. The janitor came and opened up the doors. I stepped inside and thought 'maybe …', but there were the ovens, the wilted flowers and the refrigerator rooms. I ran out into the courtyard for air!

I said to the janitor, 'well let's get some of the old blueprints of the building', and the janitor had them. We rolled the plans out and I could see that there were potentially large spaces. So we began to work on it.

Rash Sensei, Copenhagen The hard thing in dance is to practice! This is hard and takes time, the thinking is hard and the physicality is very hard.

'Our dancers don't have to be smart'
Vita Khlopova, Moscow

Moiseyev Dance Company hadn't created any new works for about 30 years, and I had danced them all. I have a typical 'Russian' face, I'm not too tall, I am flexible, so I had 'my' dances. I danced Italian dances, and tango and things like this. But once I realised I had danced it all, and I realised that for the next 20 years I would be dancing the same thing, I was bored. I chose at this point to go to university.

At this time in the Moiseyev Dance Company it was not an easy thing to go to university while you were a dancer. The director of the company, she said that I had to choose between the university and the dance company. I said, 'why? I dance from 10a.m. until 3p.m., and then after that I can go to the university, I will never miss a class, so why is it a problem?'

She said, 'our dancers don't have to be smart'.

It was really humiliating.

This mentality is a big problem. I found that the company management never tell you that you are the best dancer or that they chose you because you were the right one for the company, rather they say 'we choose you because we put an announcement out on the street, you are nobody, you just dance'.

I think this is why I quit dancing, because I didn't believe in myself, I thought I was the worst dancer in the world. I entered the university secretly, I was working and dancing six days per week, I only had Sunday as a day off and it was really a tough time. It is hard to do when you are like 17 years old!

Have you ever been on the moon?
Volker Eisenach, Berlin

Royston Muldoom came up to me and said, 'Volker, have you ever considered becoming a dancer?'

I was like, 'what?! Umm, no I hadn't'.

I was just about to finish school, and there are no artists in my family. The question was a shock; it was like being asked, 'have you ever been on the moon?'

I went home and I thought about it a bit more. I thought, 'I love dancing, but I am not the best in the group', I thought I would have to be in the front row of class all the time. I kept thinking, 'no, that is a strange question, I can't become a dancer'.

Allowing people to breathe
Gosia Mielech, Poznań

Thinking about what is happening in Europe right now, I think artists will have a very important role to play. Because artists are the ones who are saying the truth, bringing hope and also allowing people to breathe.

With the changes happening in Europe, I don't think many of the international exchanges will happen anymore. I am afraid that everywhere in Europe, art will suffer a lot, because art needs support, and I don't think the funds for these exchanges and collaborations will continue.

It makes me feel a little bit uneasy about the future. At the same time, I think that the harder the circumstances are, the more drive and passion you find inside yourself to fight for achieving your goals.

9

Travelling

A tourist
Satoshi Kudo, Stockholm

My history with Sweden has been difficult. I worked in Japan, then New York and then I moved to Stockholm with my girlfriend. We tried to find an apartment in Stockholm, but you have to wait in this long line for an apartment, you don't just get one. In five years I moved 20 times, during this time I had some work in Copenhagen, so I moved there too, but that is not included in this 20 times! So it was quite tough.

The hard thing was that as a foreign dancer, coming to the Swedish dance scene without going through Cullberg Ballet or Royal Swedish Ballet you are not invited for the freelance scene. It is almost like you are a tourist, and it was almost like I did not have a passport.

I did auditions, but each time it was like, 'who is this Japanese guy? Who is Satoshi?'

Give me wine
Elwira Piorun, Warsaw

It was very difficult to leave Poland during communist times, but the Polish National Ballet company would travel around Europe, the United States and South America.

As dancers in the company we were hardly paid, we had no money, but travelling abroad gave us a perspective on what was happening around the world. The currency exchange meant that the per diem we were given when travelling was not even enough to go to a restaurant abroad.

One of the benefits of travelling was that we had support from Polish people living abroad, because they knew the situation was bad here. In each place we went to there would be the Polish community that would do everything to make us feel like kings and queens, they would invite us to big dinners and host parties for us.

I was a soloist in the ballet company so I was especially spoilt. People would give me wine and treat me nicely.

Working like hell
Anamet Magven, Læsø

I went to London when I was 17, this was around 1992 or 1993. There I went to Pineapple Dance Studio, in Covent Garden. I didn't have much time free, I lived out in Stanmore and it was a long trip into the studio to take a class.

I did some classes and I was just blown away. I was standing behind everyone at the very back of the room, and it was filled with all of these MTV dancers looking so fancy. Of course I had quite good training, I could do high jumps and my footwork was well worked out. But of course my rhythmic flow of the movement was not good, and I was like 'what is going on?'

I was working like hell, and I enjoyed it.

Comfortable in the discomfort
Alexa Wilson, Berlin

I left New Zealand and came to Berlin because I felt like I needed to grow. I felt that I had hit a wall, and it was a feeling of stagnation. I needed to challenge myself and go into the unknown and see what is out there.

I think what is interesting for me in the moving between places is that something is constantly destabilised, like this fertile, liminal space, which can be very uncomfortable but it can also be incredibly creative and productive, and all sorts of things you never would have expected emerge.

Many people are happy to be comfortable and secure, but I am not one of those people. This feeling of 'oh I am almost comfortable in the discomfort' is something I realised before I left New Zealand. I generate discomfort for myself in making work that is vulnerable, challenging, questioning society, that's personally revealing, that's not the usual, that's risking things by crossing art forms, and doing things that might fail.

Alexa Wilson, Berlin In the early 2000s I just started to get a strange fascination with Berlin.

My life actually started at that moment
Satoshi Kudo, Stockholm

I went to New York, I was 23 years old, and I thought, 'hmm, maybe I should try Sweden?'

I found out that Cullberg Ballet had auditions in January, so I bought a ticket and went to Sweden. When I arrived it was December and it was deadly cold. In December everything in Sweden closes, there are no open classes, there wasn't anywhere to train, and I was quite depressed.

After four days I went back to New York.

Back in New York I thought, 'thank God I can still take class, I can get in shape'. So I took ballet class every day, and then finally I came back to Sweden to do the audition. I took the class with the company, it was a great experience, but after one and half hours of class, boom! That was it, I got cut.

Then my life actually started at that moment.

I thought, 'what am I going to do?'

I visited Frankfurt, I visited Amsterdam, and while travelling I thought about what I needed. I decided that I needed to learn a language first of all, because I didn't speak English well at all. I also decided that I needed to get a ballet education, a serious ballet education. So what did I do? I looked around and in that moment I thought, 'should I stay in Holland?', because I was there at the time, and they spoke English very well, and should I look for a ballet school? But I already had a professional career, so I did not feel like I wanted to go into a school, plus I was like 23 or 24, I was not young.

So I decided to go back to New York, and I studied there. Then I met a girlfriend in New York, she was in the same workshop as me, and funnily enough she was Swedish, and our relationship went on for the next 18 years. We lived in New York together, and every year I would come back to audition in Sweden at Cullberg Ballet, but I never got through.

But at one point in the United States they changed the law that meant it was hard for me to work, and everything became very hard to stay in the country, essentially you needed a green card. At the same time I lost my father, so my life was sort of at a turning point. That was why I decided to leave New York, and I came to Sweden.

Vitaly Kim, St Petersburg Right now in St Petersburg, there are a lot of foreign practices of contemporary dance – from Europe and America – that are taken and put on our dancers. We can't do it the exact same way here in Russia, we have other ways of doing things, we have different bodies, different movement impulses.

Hungarian folk dance or whatever
Anamet Magven, Læsø

I went to live in Sevilla, in the south of Spain.

I had the need to do some kind of culturally rooted dance, I had the urge to do this and it could have been Hungarian folk dance or whatever, but at this time I was fascinated with this work around the spine in flamenco.

I went to Sevilla, and I integrated flamenco into my vocabulary. I think it is still there somehow.

Spoilt for choice
Gosia Mielech, Poznań

I really appreciate the moment in history that I am in right now, being in the EU. The fact that I can travel so easily, I can fly easily across borders between countries. Poland has so many foreign choreographers coming here all the time, in the past it was impossible.

Gosia Mielech, Poznań The process and the journey of making dance is the most important for me, that is when the magic happens.

Right now, we have many dance workshops; I can even say that we are spoilt for choice. Only a few years ago, we would have two workshops a year, now there are many every week and the competition is great.

Dancing naked and singing
Elwira Piorun, Warsaw

At the end of the 1970s there was much more freedom to travel, and the ballet company from Poland travelled a lot. This meant that some of the dancers stayed abroad. There is one very famous Polish ballerina from this time who ended up dancing in the Moulin Rouge – from the ballet stage here, to dancing naked and singing in Paris!

Freezing cold
Özen Erdinc, Malmö

When I went to Helsinki I was 18 going on 19; it was close to Christmas, in December '88. Basically my whole class from the Royal Swedish Ballet School went to an open audition to the Finnish National Ballet. It was at the old Alexander Theatre.

We took the Viking Line, and we came off the boat and it was freezing cold. We thought we were in Siberia, and this was just from Stockholm to Helsinki! As I came out of the boat I saw the Uspenski Cathedral and the Senate Square. It felt so Russian, in the architecture, the ambience and the air, and it was just across the Baltic Sea from Stockholm.

Wrong language in the wrong place
Modjgan Hashemian, Berlin

I was born in Berlin and as a child I travelled back and forth from Berlin to Tehran. I learnt German, and when my family went back to Iran I couldn't understand a word of Farsi, so I always had to read from body language what was going on. I think this gave me the ability, and also the passion, to read movements. I was also expressing myself through my own body. It was like I was always with the wrong language in the wrong place, every time I started to talk and understand we moved again.

Still cooking
Susanne Frederiksen, Copenhagen

I met two people in my jazz ballet class – Christine and Kim – and they pressured me to go with them to the audition for the London Contemporary Dance School. So we all went and did the audition. We all got in and moved to London in 1980. It was the wild punk era time of London. I was a little bit punkie – I had short hair!

I stayed there for three years and had all these wonderful teachers who had actually been with Martha Graham – like Jane Dudley and Nina Fonaroff – so it was not Martha herself, but it was the next generation and quite close to the roots.

We would stand up when the teachers appeared in class, they then said, 'please be seated'. Then we had these fantastic musicians, tabla players, and pianists playing for our classes. It was so cool.

The moment I arrived
Alexa Wilson, Berlin

I worked for this woman, Linda Montano, who's a performance artist from the '80s. She's like an endurance performance artist. I worked with her from the moment I arrived in New York and we did this endurance overnight performance. So this was my arrival to New York, I had never been there and it was such an incredible introduction to the city.

A job in a café
Veera Lamberg, Helsinki

When I finished my high school education I applied for many professional dance schools. I thought that Finland is quite a small country, and I wanted to see more of the world, so I applied for Trinity Laban Conservatoire of Music and Dance in London and I got in. I was really happy.

I enjoyed the training. I think it was the right thing for me because I am also really interested in the academic way of thinking. Laban had really good balance and they encouraged academic studies.

I graduated from Laban, and I felt a little bit homesick and I wanted to come back to Finland. Of course it is also quite difficult to live in London because it is quite expensive and I didn't want to take a job in a café, I really wanted to dance. I had contacts in Finland so I thought it would be easier to start in Helsinki.

Veera Lamberg, Helsinki The best feeling in performance is when you don't need to think about the movement, and you can really try to add your own interpretation.

Visiting underground performances
Modjgan Hashemian, Berlin

In the past it was always that I went to Tehran because it was too hard for Iranian artists to come here to Germany. We were not able to do very 'real' exchanges in a physical way because of a lot of restrictions Iranians have. They cannot easily travel, this is a fact we have had to face several times.

To navigate this challenge I was teaching in Tehran, giving workshops, visiting underground performances and meeting with artists who would send me their pieces to watch by video and we would talk about them, or I would send them productions I have been producing here in Berlin.

'Hands, hands, hands'
Oxana Bellamy, Helsinki

My motivation to go to Cuba was mainly for the dancing. I always wanted to go to Cuba because my mum told me that her friend went to Cuba and said that the people there were always so happy, dancing and singing.

I had a Cuban teacher and she said to me, 'let's go with a small group', and she could help me to meet with top teachers from Havana, teachers of Afro and rumba dances. I thought 'why not?'

I went, and for me this trip was very crucial because I learnt so much. One of the teachers I had in Cuba gave such professional advice. For example, she told me, 'Oxana you are using too much energy, you have to save it'. She told me also 'hands, hands, hands' and I realised that I have to take care with my hands, that I have to use the right energy, and that I have to take care of the small steps and details.

She corrected me, and as soon as I started looking and concentrating on what the teacher was telling me things became much better with my dancing.

A stick to beat us!
Liva Zorgenfreija, Riga

I have been trained in the Russian style of ballet. When I was living in the UK I noticed that they pay attention to totally different things in ballet class. In the Russian school even the way you think about lifting your leg is different than the way they explain things in the UK.

The first class I went to in London the teacher came up to me and said, 'you're definitely from somewhere like Russia because I can see that you are doing things we don't encourage'. It's about different placement of your feet, of your legs, and a different style.

Sometimes the Russian school is very strict and they don't care about your body so much, but I think in this Western way of dancing ballet they try to make sure that you don't hurt yourself. In the Russian school at some point our teacher's end up walking around with a stick to beat us!

All the ABBA songs
Özen Erdinc, Malmö

I have memories of taking cruises from Helsinki to Stockholm. On these trips there would be midnight shows, and they had different themes every time, and of course, as a dancer, you look at these shows with a certain eye.

There were all kinds of themes to the performances, samba, ABBA where they would sing and perform all the ABBA songs, Irish dancing and Spanish salsa. When I took the trip with my dance friends we always had so much fun. I always told them that we have to be nice, and not to look at the performers in the show with a critical eye; we have to remember that they are entertainers. You can see that the crowd, normal people who aren't dancers, they all love it – it's such a great show, the music, and the feathers.

I have been in less calm boat rides across the Baltic over the years, and I have been in a few storms, where they actually had to cancel the shows on the boats because of the risk of the dancers twisting their ankles.

Profound home stories
Jo Parkes, Berlin

I had come back to London from Los Angeles and I was feeling very dislocated. I was surrounded by kids from all over the world, and I thought it would be really interesting for us to look at the idea of 'home'.

Over a long period of time I made a film called *Home*, with young people and their families in the East End of London. I didn't choose who was going to be in the film, but rather I did a series of open workshops and the young people chose if they wanted to be involved or not. Of course the young people who chose to come had very profound home stories, so we started to work.

That was the first time that I had contact with young people who had arrived in a country as refugees, and a lot of them were from the Balkans at that time because of war, some of the same stories as now unfortunately.

The Wild West
Krysztof Fijak, Otrebusy

Going on tour to North America was a long tour, it was about three or four months in total. It was in 1985 and was 101 days and 86 performances, we went to all the states in the USA, from south to north, from New York to California, including the Wild West!

We travelled by bus, and sometimes by plane. I remember one performance because the theatre was very famous, it was at Carnegie Hall in New York, and we performed there for four nights. We stayed at the Wellington Hotel, one street away from the theatre and we would just walk to the theatre. It was a good time.

A time difference
Cher Geurtze, Copenhagen

I got an invitation to come to Denmark from a friend, Rhea Leman. I had been working with her in the United States and she had said to me, 'come over, we can do some shows'.

I had never been out of America; I had never flown before; I didn't have a passport, all those kinds of things. I didn't even know there was a time difference.

I wrote in letters to my girlfriend who was picking me up at the airport in Copenhagen, 'I'll be there on the 26th of the month', but that was actually the day I was leaving America and I got here on the 27th of the month – these were the days before the internet and I didn't have a clue about anything!

In the right place
Raivis Dzjamko, Riga

I went to a summer dance school in France. There I discovered jazz dance, and I felt like I had found something that allowed me to be free. I did the two weeks of the summer school and then they asked me to stay to study in this professional jazz school. The tuition would be free; I just had to find somewhere to live.

At this time I did not speak English, I did not speak French, and I had no money. But I thought why not? I will stay and take a risk. It was a time in my life where everything was in the right place.

The night before I left Latvia for France I moved from my apartment, I had paid all my debts, it was like I was free from everything. I thought well, there is nothing in Latvia holding me back, I really should go.

Cherishing women
Oxana Bellamy, Helsinki

After two years of solo dancing I went to Cuba and I saw people dancing socially in the evenings. In the parties men were inviting women to dance – not like in Finland!

In Finland men say they are too shy, and that the women have to invite the men to dance. For me this was a shock, especially coming from the Russian culture. Men in Cuba were so happy, so polite, and like they were cherishing women. I came away from Cuba with a strong will to start partner dancing.

No one sleeps
Helmi Järvensivu, Rovaniemi

I have been living away from home for more than ten years now, so my family are used to me being far away. Though my mother still talks about me being far away and that my family hardly gets to see me.

I am originally from the south of Finland, and I do feel lots of richness here in Lapland. I find the atmosphere and people in Lapland are pretty different compared to those in southern Finland. The main difference would also be how the year goes by – in summer there's only light and no one sleeps, whereas in winter it's really dark and cold.

The seasons affect the behaviour of people who live here. During winter everyone becomes really slow and peaceful, and in summer they just do everything. We have more performances in autumn when it's dark and wet. I think it's more of a mental thing that people become more awake and have the strength to do things in summer. I feel that there's a sense of tiredness that kicks in during autumn and winter, when we come closer to December. The energy level then rises up around February, maybe due to the appearance of the light again.

Passports for my dogs
Anna Solakius, Lund

I mainly teach in Lund, where I was born, but every Tuesday, I also work at a studio in Copenhagen.

Last week when I was travelling from Copenhagen to Lund I lost my ID. The thing is right now, you can't come back to Sweden unless you have an ID, and

I lost it on the train from central Copenhagen to the airport, where I was going to change trains. I realised it when I was right in front of the guy who was going to check the documents. I thought I had put it in my pocket, but it was not there. I was standing there and I just thought, 'Shit! My ID!', and I was there with my two dogs. I have passports for my dogs! But that doesn't help. I started to realise that it was probably on the train, which was on the other side of the platform, and I just froze. I didn't know what to do. They wouldn't let me on the train without ID so I had to find a solution.

I asked someone to take my spare key to my apartment, go to my apartment, find my passport, take my car, drive over the bridge and pick me up from the airport, and that's how I could come home. It's like this right now because Sweden has decided to close the borders as there have been a lot of refugees coming.

10
Futures, challenges and questions

Integrated in society
Veera Lamberg, Helsinki

I feel that there is no point to do art just for professionals. Somehow we need a more diverse audience and we really need to get dance into lots of different places.

So that is the thing I would like to see, to see dance much more integrated in society. I think this is the key for the new audience, and for the working situation for the artists.

Break the rules
Edmundus Zicka, Vilnius

I never thought that I would do folk dance and modern dance together, or folk and retro dance together. I am interested to see where something like folk dance on a TV show could take the dance form.

I know that some of the more conservative older people involved with folk dance are worried about what might happen, and what direction folk dance could go. I think they're worried we are going to break the rules by mixing folk dance with pop and rock and all of these other things together.

Amazing and mysterious
Alexa Wilson, Berlin

If you'd asked me 20 years ago: do you think you would do half the things you have done in the past 20 years? I never would have imagined in a million years that I would have done so many of those things!

So this unfolding of life and dance in amazing and mysterious ways is a beautiful thing. But I also think the organic process it has taken has made things take longer as a result. What is both exciting and unnerving is that it is not always entirely clear what might happen next.

Go nuts to pop music
Magdalena Jankowski, Otrebusy

Sometimes when my dancing friends and I are out, and pop and house music is playing, we do some folk dance moves.

When that happens I can see that everyone in the club is like backing up and like watching what they are doing.

It happens more for fun, it is not that we are taking it seriously. It's unlikely that you're going to hear folk music these days when you are in a club or a bar, so it is sometimes just fun to go nuts to pop music.

Can run so fast
Satoshi Kudo, Stockholm

I want to take away the hierarchy of dance. Like, if you are a dancer, and you have a beautiful pointe, and there is another dancer who does not have a beautiful pointe, then there is already a divide.

Some people can run so fast, and some people cannot; some people can carry so much, and some people cannot; but it does not mean the people who cannot do something have any less value.

I do not like to see the world in this way. Everyone has a value, and every dancer has a value.

Strong and serious
Marija Kaklauskaite, Vilnius

My boyfriend and I brainstormed slowly for months and finally came up with the name for a crew – *Syndicates*. I think this name is perfect. It sounds strong and

Rash Sensei, Copenhagen My favourite time when I dance is when people understand something I am trying to convey. Those moments when I share something with people are very special.

serious. It means a group of people interested or united by one common interest. It fits us perfectly! Sadly, we haven't called ourselves that officially yet.

The idea of having a team has started to push me more to develop my skills and style. Dedication to the idea is my energy at the moment and I look forward to one day standing as a syndicate. I think the word 'syndicate' describes me and my team's character, attitude and style and it would be written on the back of our t-shirts.

This dream makes me love what I do even more and inspires me to break free from my shy self and comfort zone and to reveal who I am – charismatic, fun and a serious fighter.

A full piece
Gosia Mielech, Poznań

I haven't had a chance yet to create a full dance piece outside of Poland. Hopefully it will happen, it is out there in my dreams, so as my friends would say, it is already happening.

178 Dance, Diversity and Difference

Gosia Mielech, Poznań We sometimes forget to enjoy dancing.

'Yeah, sure it is like basketball or lifting weights'
Mindaugas (Minda) Bruzas, Vilnius

Here in Lithuania I think people still have an old mentality about dance. When you say 'dance' to someone they often think of classical ballet or folk dance. When they see what I do people will say to me, 'you spin on your head, that is not dance'. Sometimes they ask if it is like a sport. I say, 'yeah, sure it is like basketball or lifting weights, you have to train hard and work hard'.

I think now people are starting to appreciate showcases of dance, they see flips and think it is impressive, I think dance on television has something to do with this. But they don't get battles so much. I see that a younger generation gets it, but an older generation do not totally accept it.

I hope that in 20 years it will be very normal to be a hip hop dancer here in Vilnius, and people can be full-time performers. I feel like my friends and I are working on it not working for ourselves, but perhaps for the next generation so they can benefit from our work.

A little library
Modjgan Hashemian, Berlin

For my dance colleagues and friends in Tehran I am organising something called the *Suitcase of Dance*. I think it is important to do this because there is no way you can study dance formally in Iran, the only access you have is through the internet, and even that can also be limited and not everybody has this.

So I was thinking of making this suitcase full of dance-related materials – literature like books, articles and magazines, DVDs, all sorts of different things, especially about contemporary dance. I can collect this into one suitcase and take it to Iran. There are different spaces in Tehran where this could be a little library.

Of course if I travel from Germany with this suitcase there is danger involved, a risk that it could be confiscated or get me or others in trouble with Iranian authorities, but these are risks to take.

Peace as every day life
Njara Rasolo, Helsinki

I recently created an event called *Battle for Peace*.

I have been asked, 'why call it a *Battle for Peace*?'

In my opinion this is a bit of an obvious answer about why do this, with what is going on in the world now, just look around.

If you just look in Finland, yeah we are relatively well and happy here, but I want to say, 'my friend, just travel for two hours from Finland and then you will see why we need peace, if you go to Madagascar then you see why peace is needed in the world'. We need peace on a small scale, as in peace within human beings in everyday life, and we need peace on a big scale as a political decision and relationships between countries and different groups of people. I see an event like *Battle for Peace* being about the future, and who leads the future? The young people.

We know there are things going on in Syria, and many people are coming to places like Europe because they *have* to leave, they are not coming to hurt people. So the people in Europe who are receiving the new people have to be at peace with this, these people are in need, let them come and receive them with all your heart and with peace.

Something totally new
Vita Khlopova, Moscow

I think people can have their own opinion about dance, but they have to be able to tell me why they might like or not like something.

Sometimes when I give a lecture publicly people ask me 'so do you like this choreographer or that choreographer?' and I tell them 'it doesn't matter if I like them or not, I just told you their story as I know it'.

Often I think people want to know what is 'right' and 'wrong' so they can then make their choices about what to do or not do here in Russia. I think we don't need to repeat what has happened in Western Europe. Our history here in Russia is rich and unique, perhaps we can make something totally new. I think people get frustrated here sometimes, and they say, 'I give up, I am going to Europe'.

I think, 'why is Europe better?'

Keep the curiosity going
Mart Kangaro, Tallinn

A challenge I have as an artist is to understand if the questions you are asking in your work are relevant.

Of course there are political and cultural challenges, like, what kinds of position artists have in society, and how this changes over time? But I think the challenge for me is to keep the curiosity going.

I think it's totally fine to fail, I think failure is very much okay, and with time I'm not so scared of that anymore. But it is the curiosity that is vital for me to keep moving forward.

'Oh, you are just a dancer'
Veera Lamberg, Helsinki

My MA research was qualitative research about the dance situation in Finland, from the perspective of dancers. I wanted to talk to people who wanted to be dancers, as in make dancing and performing as their full-time paid job, and ask them how they find it in Finland.

One thing that was revealed was that often there is not a basic regular income and there are often short contracts, and only a few grants help dancers concentrate on their work and their artistry. Most have to teach and do so many things at the same time to make an income.

Another thing that became apparent was that in Finland there are not many open auditions, and this is a problem because everything goes through who you know. Also many of the dancers I talked to said that they really wanted to do a variety of things, not just dancing really physically demanding work, they wanted to do things that were more dramatic or experimental and things like that, but if you don't know the right people, or you've been performing in just one style of pieces, that can be difficult.

It seems like people often think, 'oh, you are just a dancer in that style' and you might not get chances in other styles of things.

Finish my dream
Satoshi Kudo, Stockholm

I am 48 years old, which is a little old for a choreographer just starting out, but I am full of hope.

I am very much enjoying being freelance, it is a lot of work, but I have to say that living in Sweden for nearly 19 years has given me a chance to finish my dream.

So as a Japanese guy, going on this long journey, it was not so bad, I must say.

A responsibility
Jo Parkes, Berlin

I was working with refugees before the current European refugee crisis hit.

I was approached by an organisation taking part in a Berlin-wide project that paired arts organisations with accommodation centres for refugees. I started to test out using dance as a form to support women and children arriving here in Germany to make first connections and to find themselves here in Berlin.

I, and the team I work with, have developed a programme we now offer in three different accommodation centres. Essentially what we have built is a pool of contemporary dance artists who go once a week in teams and dance with young people and also with women. It's really about refugees who are in a very small space and have an extraordinary need to move, but also using contemporary dance to help them root themselves, find their bodies and have a connection to each other.

As I started doing this work I understood the first six months is really about finding a way to manage the dynamics of the groups, because a lot of the young people are not well looked after at the moment because their parents are traumatised and very busy standing in line at different authorities dealing with bureaucracy. The youth have a lot of time to hang around, they come from different countries and cultures that might also be in conflict with each other, and they are all living together. There is an extraordinary amount of violence; the aggression is very near the surface – physically, emotionally and verbally.

Originally I felt like it was and should be a closed process of working together. Then as the whole Pegida theme started to emerge and as that gathered momentum I understood that actually I had a responsibility to try to communicate something to people outside of what we were doing in the centres. But the big issue in the work that I do is how do you do that without exploiting people?

Full of surprises
Oxana Bellamy, Helsinki

I think the worst thing in life would be when you are dying and lying in bed thinking, 'oh, I wish I had tried to dance'.

That is why if people want to dance they should just go and dance. Because you never know what might happen, life is full of surprises.

The one day that you go and start dancing might just be the day that turns your life around completely.

Oxana Bellamy, Helsinki I would like to tell other people that if they want to experience dance they don't need to be shy to try.

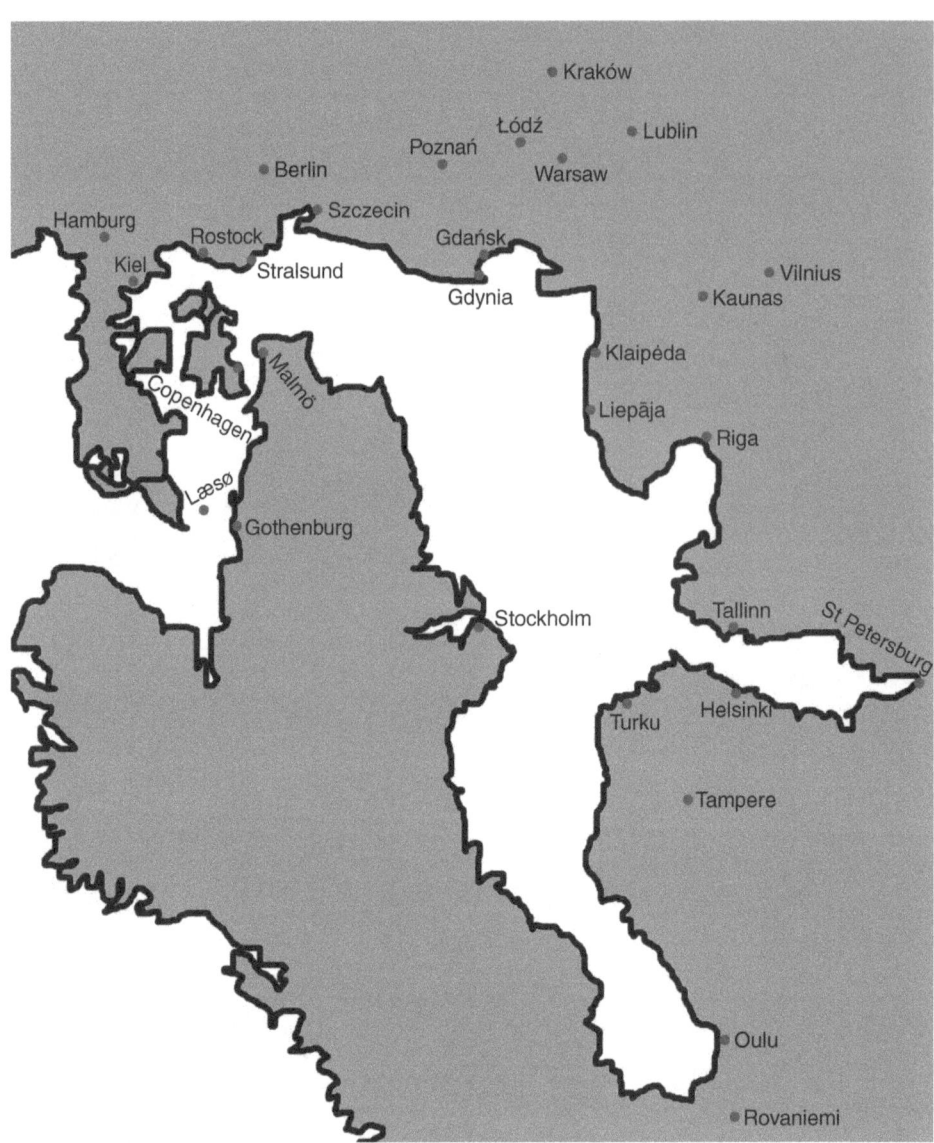

The Baltic Sea

List of interviewees

Alyona. Dancer, STAGE Dance Theatre. Interview conducted by Rose Martin in Russian with translation by Katerina Urbanovich in St Petersburg on 18 July 2016.
Bellamy, Oxana. Dancer. Interview conducted by Rose Martin in English in Helsinki on 8 June 2016.
Bruzas, Mindaugas. Dancer, Skillz Dance Studio. Interview conducted by Rose Martin in English in Vilnius on 13 February 2016.
Ceponis, Antanas Tony. Dancer, Skillz Dance Studio. Interview conducted by Rose Martin in English in Vilnius on 13 February 2016.
Claus, Santa. Public figure. Interview conducted by Nicholas Rowe in English in Rovaniemi on 14 February 2016.
Dzjamko, Raivis. Dancer and teacher, Dzirnas. Interview conducted by Rose Martin in English in Riga on 15 February 2016.
Eisenach, Volker. Choreographer, dance educator and director, Faster-Than-Light Dance Company. Interview conducted by Rose Martin in English in Berlin on 4 February 2016.
Erdinc, Özen. Dancer. Interview conducted by Nicholas Rowe in English in Malmö on 6 February 2016.
Fijak, Krysztof. Dancer, Mazowsze Dance Ensemble. Interview conducted by Rose Martin in English in Otrebusy on 7 July 2016.
Frederiksen, Susanne. Dance educator. Interview conducted by Rose Martin in English in Copenhagen on 19 June 2016.
Geurtze, Cher. Dance educator and director, Dansekapellet. Interview conducted by Rose Martin in English in Copenhagen on 20 June 2016.
Gröndahl, Ella. Dance student. Interview conducted by Nicholas Rowe in English in Oulu on 12 February 2016.
Hashemian, Modjgan. Dancer and choreographer. Interview conducted by Rose Martin in English in Berlin on 1 July 2016.
Herd, Atte. Dancer, Dance Theatre Rimpparemmi. Interview conducted by Nicholas Rowe in English in Rovaniemi on 15 February 2016.
Höckner, Simone. Dancer. Interview conducted by Nicholas Rowe in English in Malmö on 6 February 2016.
Hoikma, Nina. Dancer. Interview conducted by Nicholas Rowe in English in Rovaniemi on 14 February 2016.

Jaakonaho, Liisa. Dance educator and PhD candidate, University of the Arts Helsinki. Interview conducted by Rose Martin in English in Helsinki on 8 June 2016.

Jankauskas, Vytis. Choreographer and director. Interview conducted by Rose Martin in Lithuanian with translation by Giedre Jankauskiene in Vilnius on 13 February 2016.

Jankowski, Magdalena. Dancer, Mazowsze Dance Ensemble. Interview conducted by Kendall Jones by Skype on 21 December 2017.

Järvensivu, Helmi. Dancer, Dance Theatre Rimpparemmi. Interview conducted by Nicholas Rowe in English in Rovaniemi on 15 February 2016.

Kaklauskaite, Marija. Dancer, Skillz Dance Studio. Interview conducted by Rose Martin in English in Vilnius on 13 February 2016.

Kangaro, Mart. Dancer and choreographer. Interview conducted by Kendall Jones in English by Skype on 19 January 2017.

Kasparov, Vadim. Manager, Kannon Dance House and Open Look Dance Festival. Interview conducted by Rose Martin in English in St Petersburg on 18 July 2016.

Khlopova, Vita. Dance scholar and researcher, No Fixed Points. Interview conducted by Rose Martin in English in St Petersburg on 20 July 2016.

Kim, Eveniya. Manager, STAGE Dance Theatre. Interview conducted by Rose Martin in Russian with translation by Katerina Urbanovich in St Petersburg on 18 July 2016.

Kim, Vitaly. Director, STAGE Dance Theatre. Interview conducted by Rose Martin in Russian with translation by Katerina Urbanovich in St Petersburg on 18 July 2016.

Kudo, Satoshi. Dancer, teacher and choreographer. Interview conducted by Rose Martin in English in Stockholm on 14 June 2016.

Lamberg, Veera. Dancer, teacher and choreographer. Interview conducted by Rose Martin in English in Helsinki on 29 July 2016.

Lohi, Laura. Dancer, Skånes Dansteater. Interview conducted by Nicholas Rowe in English in Malmö on 5 February 2016.

Magven, Anamet. Dancer, choreographer and dance educator. Interview conducted by Rose Martin in English in Copenhagen on 23 June 2016.

Mielech, Gosia. Dancer, teacher and choreographer, DanceLab. Interview conducted by Rose Martin in English in Poznań on 8 July 2016.

Milczuk, Wioletta. Dancer, Mazowsze Dance Ensemble. Interview conducted by Rose Martin in Polish with translation by Marta Pokrywczyńska in Otrebusy on 7 July 2016.

Parkes, Jo. Freelance dance/video artist, Jo Parkes Mobile Dance. Interview conducted by Rose Martin in English in Berlin on 31 January 2016.

Paś, Anna. Dancer, Mazowsze Dance Ensemble. Interview conducted by Rose Martin in Polish with translation by Marta Pokrywczyńska in Otrebusy on 7 July 2016.

Patsey, Anastasia. Artist and director, Museum for Non-Conformist Art. Interview conducted by Rose Martin in English in St Petersburg on 19 July 2016.

Pilhjarta, Anni. Dancer, Dance Theatre Rimpparemmi. Interview conducted by Nicholas Rowe in English in Rovaniemi on 15 February 2016.

Piorun, Elwira. Dance teacher and director, Teatr Tańca Zawirowania. Interview conducted by Rose Martin in Polish with translation by Iwona Wojnicka in Warsaw on 7 February 2016.

Rantanen, Maija. Dancer. Interview conducted by Rose Martin in English in Helsinki on 10 June 2016.

Rasolo, Njara. Dancer, teacher and choreographer. Interview conducted by Rose Martin in English in Helsinki on 9 July 2016.

Raszewska, Hanna. Dance researcher and scholar, Fryderyk Chopin University of Music and Mazowiecki Instytut Kultury. Interview conducted by Rose Martin in English in Warsaw on 6 February 2016.

Sensei, Rash. Dancer, La Folie Crew. Interview conducted by Rose Martin in Copenhagen on 20 June 2016.

Solakius, Anna. Tango teacher and dancer. Interview conducted by Nicholas Rowe in English in Lund on 4 February 2016.

Steinam, Uldim. Director, Vektors Folk Dance Ensemble. Interview conducted by Rose Martin in Latvian with translation by Iluta Goba in Riga on 15 February 2016.

Studens, Petezis. Dancer, Vektors Folk Dance Ensemble. Interview conducted by Rose Martin in English in Riga on 15 February 2016.

Urbanovich, Katerina. Dancer, STAGE Dance Theatre. Interview conducted by Rose Martin in English in St Petersburg on 18 July 2016.

Vahtola, Niina. Teacher at the University of Oulu. Interview conducted by Nicholas Rowe in English in Oulu on 13 February 2016.

Westerlund, Moa. Freelance dancer. Interview conducted by Rose Martin in English in Stockholm on 14 June 2016.

Wilson, Alexa. Dancer and choreographer. Interview conducted by Rose Martin in English in Berlin on 2 July 2016.

Wojnicka, Iwona. Dancer and choreographer, Format Zero. Interview conducted by Rose Martin in English in Warsaw on 6 February 2016.

Zalipska, Magdalena. Dancer, Mazowsze Dance Ensemble. Interview conducted by Rose Martin in Polish with translation by Marta Pokrywczyńska in Otrebusy on 7 July 2016.

Zalipski, Piotr. Dancer, Mazowsze Dance Ensemble. Interview conducted by Rose Martin in English in Otrebusy on 7 July 2016.

Zicka, Edmundus. Dancer and director, Sietuva Dance Company. Interview conducted by Rose Martin in English in Vilnius on 13 February 2016.

Zorgenfreija, Liva. Dancer, Vektors Folk Dance Ensemble. Interview conducted by Rose Martin in English in Riga on 15 February 2016.

List of references

Anderson, B. (1991). *Imagined Communities: Reflections on the Origins and Spread of Nationalism*. New York: Verso.
Asad, T. (1973). *Anthropology and the Colonial Encounter*. Amherst, NY: Humanity Books.
Boal, A. (1985). *Theatre of the Oppressed*. New York: Theatre Communication Group.
—— (1992). *Games for Actors and Non-actors*. London: Routledge.
Bunce, V. (1985). 'The empire strikes back: The evolution of the Eastern bloc from a Soviet asset to a Soviet liability'. *International Organization*, 39(1), pp.1–46.
Castañeda, Q.E. (2006). 'The invisible theatre of ethnography: Performative principles of fieldwork'. *Anthropological Quarterly*, 79(1), pp.75–104.
Cerwonka, A. and Malkki, L.H. (2008). *Improvising Theory: Process and Temporality in Ethnographic Fieldwork*. Chicago: University of Chicago Press.
Chatterjee, P. (1993). *The Nation and its Fragments: Colonial and Postcolonial Histories*. Princeton, NJ: Princeton University Press.
Connelly, F.M. and Clandinin, D.J. (1990). 'Stories of experience and narrative inquiry'. *Educational Researcher*, 19(5), pp.2–14.
Davis, L.E. (2015). *The Cold War Begins: Soviet–American Conflict over East Europe*. Princeton, NJ: Princeton University Press.
Falzon, M.A. (ed.). (2016). *Multi-sited Ethnography: Theory, Praxis and Locality in Contemporary Research*. Abingdon, Oxon: Routledge.
Ferguson, R. (2009). *The Vikings: A History*. New York: Penguin Books.
Ginkel, J. (2002). 'Identity construction in Latvia's 'singing revolution': Why inter-ethnic conflict failed to occur'. *Nationalities Papers*, 30(3), pp.403–33.
Hamm, P., King, L.P. and Stuckler, D. (2012). 'Mass privatization, state capacity, and economic growth in post-communist countries'. *American Sociological Review*, 77(2), pp.295–324.
Heyl, B.S. (2001). 'Ethnographic interviewing'. In P. Atkinson, A. Coffey, S. Delmont, J. Lofland and L. Lofland (eds), *Handbook of Ethnography* (pp.204–19). London: Sage.
Hobsbawm, E. and Ranger, T. (eds). (1983). *The Invention of Tradition*. Cambridge, UK: Cambridge University Press.
Huntington, S.P. (1997). *The Clash of Civilizations and the Remaking of World Order*. New York: Touchstone.

Jansson, B.O. (2003). 'The Baltic Sea'. In K. Sherman and G. Hempel (eds), *Large Marine Ecosystems of the World Trends in Exploitation, Protection and Research* (pp.148–70). Amsterdam: Elsevier.

Lane, T., Pabriks, A., Purs, A. and Smith, D.J. (2013). *The Baltic States: Estonia, Latvia and Lithuania*. Abingdon, Oxon: Routledge.

Lewis, B. (2002). *What went Wrong?: Western Impact and Middle Eastern Response*. Oxford: Oxford University Press.

Maciejewski, W. (2002). *The Baltic Sea Region: Cultures, Politics, Societies*. Uppsala: Baltic University Press.

Mack, J. (2013). *The Sea: A Cultural History*. London: Reaktion Books.

Marcus, G.E. (1995). 'Ethnography in/of the world system: The emergence of multi-sited ethnography'. *Annual Review of Anthropology*, 24(1), pp.95–117.

—— (1998). *Ethnography through Thick and Thin*. Princeton, NJ: Princeton University Press.

Melnikas, B. (2008). 'The new case of transformations in the European Union: Integral space creation processes in the Baltic Region'. *Viesoji Politika ir Administravimas*, (24), pp.9–24.

Mouritzen, H. (1993). 'The two musterknaben and the naughty boy: Sweden, Finland and Denmark in the process of European integration'. *Cooperation and Conflict*, 28(4), pp.373–402.

North, M. (2015). *The Baltic: A History*. Cambridge, MA: Harvard University Press.

Palmer, A. (2007). *The Baltic: A New History of the Region and its People*. London: The Overlook Press.

Pfeifer, C., Smolny, W. and Wagner, J. (2016). '25 Years of German reunification'. *Jahrbücher für Nationalökonomie und Statistik*, 236(2), pp.153–5.

Prakash, G. (1990). 'Writing post-orientalist histories of the Third World: Perspectives from Indian historiography'. *Comparative Studies in Society and History*, 32(2), pp.383–408.

Razum, O. and Bozorgmehr, K. (2015). 'Disgrace at EU's external borders'. *International Journal of Public Health*, 60(5), pp.515–16.

Saarikoski, H. (2014). *Silloin tanssittiin tangoa: Tanssikansan kertomaa 1900-luvulta (Back then we Danced the Tango: Tales by Dance Folks from the 1900s)*. Helsinki, Finland: Partuuna.

Said, E. (1978). *Orientalism*. New York: Vintage Press.

Sarotte, M.E. (2014). *1989: The Struggle to Create post-Cold War Europe*. Princeton, NJ: Princeton University Press.

Sawyer, R.K. (2000). 'Improvisation and the creative process: Dewey, Collingwood, and the aesthetics of spontaneity'. *The Journal of Aesthetics and Art Criticism*, 58(2), pp.149–61.

Shay, A. (1999). 'Parallel traditions: State folk dance ensembles and folkdance in the field'. *Dance Research Journal*, 31(1), pp.29–56.

Šmidchens, G. (2007). 'National heroic narratives in the Baltics as a source for nonviolent political action'. *Slavic Review*, 66(3), pp.484–508.

—— (2014). *The Power of Song: Nonviolent National Culture in the Baltic Singing Revolution*. Washington: University of Washington Press.

Stokes, G. (1993). *The Walls Came Tumbling Down: The Collapse of Communism in Eastern Europe*. Oxford: Oxford University Press.

Thomson, C. (1992). *The Singing Revolution: A Political Journey through the Baltic States*. Harmondsworth: Michael Joseph.

Trotsky, L. and Eastman, M. (2008). *History of the Russian Revolution*. Chicago, IL: Haymarket Books.

Tuhiwai Smith, L. (1999). *Decolonizing Methodologies: Research and Indigenous Peoples*. Dunedin: University of Otago Press.

UNESCO. (2011). *Seoul Agenda: Goals for the Development of Arts Education*. Available at http://www.unesco.org/new/en/culture/themes/creativity/arts-education/official-texts/development-goals/ (accessed 25 November 2016).

Vesilind, P., Tusty, J. and Tusty, M. (2008). *The Singing Revolution: How Culture Saved a Nation*. Tallinn: Varrak.

Voipio, A. (1981). *The Baltic Sea* (Vol. 30). New York: Elsevier.

Wæver, O. (1992). 'Nordic nostalgia: Northern Europe after the Cold War'. *International Affairs (Royal Institute of International Affairs 1944–)*, 68(1), pp.77–102.

Winroth, A. (2014). *The Age of the Vikings*. Princeton, NJ: Princeton University Press.

Glossary

dabke – A folk dance that is popular in locations such as Palestine, Lebanon, Syria, Iraq, Jordan, the north of Saudi Arabia, occupied Palestinian territories/Israel and Yemen. The dance is often performed at weddings and celebrations; however, it is also performed in theatrical or contemporary modes.

DDR – The state of East Germany that was formally called the Deutsche Demokratische Republik (abbreviated as DDR), and was a former state in Europe from 1949–1990.

dyskinesia – An abnormality or impairment of voluntary movement.

EU – The European Union was founded in 1993, and is a union of 28 member states located primarily in Europe.

fouettés – A ballet movement of a pirouette performed with a quarter circular whipping movement of the raised leg to the side. Fouettés are usually performed multiple times within a balletic context, often by women wearing pointe shoes.

Gaga – A movement language that was developed by Ohad Naharin, in parallel to his work as a choreographer and the artistic director of Batsheva Dance Company.

hal tatakallam Alearabia? – Translates from Arabic as 'do you speak Arabic?'.

Iron Curtain – A notional barrier separating the former Soviet bloc and the West prior to the decline of communism that followed the political events in eastern Europe in 1989.

KGB – Komitet Gosudarstvennoy Bezopasnosti (abbreviated as KGB) was the main security agency for the Soviet Union from 1954 until 1991.

mañana – Translates from Spanish as 'tomorrow' or 'specified future time'.

mujeres – Translates from Spanish as 'women'.

Nevsky Prospect – A main street in the city of St Petersburg, Russia.

orishas – A spirit that reflects one of the manifestations of the supreme divinities in the Yoruba religion. Percussion is a crucial component of the religion, in that it is the vehicle through which devotees communicate with the orishas (deities). For the most important religious ceremonies, an ensemble of three double-headed batá drums is employed and frequently augmented by the acheré (a small gourd rattle).

pas de bourrée – A transitional movement in ballet in which the dancer transfers body weight quickly from foot to foot in three small steps.

Pegida – Patriotic Europeans Against the Islamisation of the West (abbreviated PEGIDA or Pegida) is a nationalist, anti-Islam, far-right political movement, founded in Dresden, Germany, in October 2014.

pirouettes – A balletic turn on one foot.

pliés – A bending of the knee or knees in ballet, also a term used in other dance styles such as modern and contemporary dance practices.

relevés – A movement in ballet in which the dancer rises on the tips of the toes if wearing pointe shoes, or onto the ball of the foot if wearing soft shoes.

shukran jazilaan – Translates from Arabic as 'thank you a lot'.

son – A genre of Cuban popular music, also known as son cubano.

son montuno – A subgenre of son cubano music.

tabla – A large, cylindrical double-sided drum, played with the hand on one side and with a beater on the other.

USSR – The Union of Soviet Socialist Republics was a socialist state that existed from 1922 until 1991.

Vaganova style – The Vaganova method or style is a ballet technique and training system devised by the Russian dancer and pedagogue Agrippina Vaganova.

waldkindergarten – Translates from German to 'forest kindergarten', and is a type of preschool education for children between the ages of approximately three and six years old that is held almost entirely outdoors. Within this education model children are encouraged to play, explore and learn in a forest or natural environment.

Notes

Introduction

1. Far right ultra nationalist/anti-immigrant groups include the Patriotic Europeans Against the Islamisation of the West, Latvian Fatherland and Freedom Party, Estonian Conservative National Party, The True Finns Party, Liberal Democratic Party of Russia, Order and Justice Party Lithuania and the Nordic Resistance Movement. Other groups contributing to this far right perspective include various anti-immigrant street patrol groups such as the Soldiers of Odin in Finland.
2. The terms axis and allies in relation to World War II (1939–45) refers to the axis powers of Germany, Italy, Japan, Hungary, Romania, and Bulgaria versus Allies of the US, Britain, France, USSR, Australia, Belgium, Brazil, Canada, China, Denmark, Greece, Netherlands, New Zealand, Norway, Poland, South Africa and Yugoslavia.
3. The Singing Revolution refers to events between 1987 and 1991 that led to the independence of Estonia, Latvia and Lithuania from the USSR (Ginkel, 2002; Vesilind, Tusty and Tusty, 2008). The term was coined by an Estonian activist and artist, Heinz Valk, in an article published in June 1988, a week after the spontaneous mass night-singing demonstrations at the Tallinn Song Festival Grounds (Smidchens, 2014). During this time there was also the Baltic Chain, a peaceful political demonstration on 23 August 1989. The Baltic Chain involved approximately 2 million people who joined hands to form a human chain extending 600 kilometres across Latvia, Lithuania and Estonia (Ginkel, 2002).

Index

10 Pushkinskaya 145–6

ABBA 171
Afghanistan 115
African dance 92, 110
Afro-Rap 91–2
Alexander Theatre 167
Alice in Wonderland 95
American dance 6, 72–3, 118, 172
American Embassy 73
Amsterdam 165
Anonymous 65–6
Arctic Circle 7, 95
Art Space 79
Auckland 14, 79
Austria 79

Bachata 92
Baker, Josephine 119
Baku 133
Balanchine, George 86
Balkans 115, 171
ballet 3, 6, 21, 23–4, 28, 30–3, 36–8, 41,
    43, 46, 49–53, 55, 59–60, 66, 77, 81,
    84, 86, 98, 103–4, 110–12, 118–21,
    124–5, 128–31, 133–4, 140, 143,
    146, 148, 150, 152–4, 156–7, 162–5,
    167–8, 170–1, 178
Barcelona 44
Battle for Peace 179
Bausch, Pina 32, 33
Béjart, Maurice 119
Berkeley College 71

Berlin/West Berlin 1–2, 6, 28–9, 32, 34,
    44, 46, 50, 53–5, 61–3, 67, 69,
    75–8, 93, 99, 101, 107, 111–12,
    114–17, 123, 128, 131, 137–8, 140,
    144–7, 151–2, 155, 159, 161,
    163–4, 167–8, 170–1, 176,
    179, 181
Berlin Wall 137, 146
Berliner Philharmoniker 159
bhangra 99
Bispebjerg 175
Bolshoi 38, 49, 53, 55, 119,
    128, 143
Boston 71
Bournonville 77
breakdancing 20, 88
Butoh 39, 56, 80, 98

Café Muller 33
California 172
Candoco 120
Carnegie Hall 172
Centre National de la Danse 49
Chan, Jackie 22
Chechnya 115
Christmas 95, 159, 167
Comaneci, Nadia 27
communism 25
Congo 64, 88, 126
Copenhagen 28, 30, 50, 55, 60, 64, 69–70,
    73, 88, 91, 105, 108, 110, 112, 114,
    116, 118, 120, 126, 128–9, 159–60,
    162, 168, 172–4, 177

corps de ballet 53
Covent Garden 163
Crutchfield, Doug 50
Cuba/Cuban 21, 30, 54, 92, 114, 142, 154, 155, 170, 173
Cuban orishas 21
Cuban rumba 21, 154, 170
Cullberg Ballet 104, 124, 153, 162, 164–5
Cunningham, Merce 49, 74

dabke 156
daCi 6
Dance House 148
DanceLab 125
Dans in Nordvest 159
Denishawn 118
Denmark/Danish 7–9, 22, 60, 64, 88, 105, 109–10, 120, 172
Deutsche Demokratische Republik 145
Diaghilev, Sergei 49
Dresden 144–5
Dublin 95
Dudley, Jane 168
Duisburg 54
Duncan, Isadora 118–19

Ek, Mats 64, 104, 153
Ekman, Alexander 104
End 124
England/English 1, 13, 32, 55, 58, 73, 101, 103, 109, 120, 154, 172
Espoo 21, 44, 52, 89–90, 126, 138, 142, 154
EU 10, 166
Europe/European/Western Europe/Central Europe/Eastern Europe 2–4, 6–7, 9–10, 52, 63, 65, 71, 78, 92, 118–19, 138, 140, 152, 161–2, 165, 179–81
Eurovision Song Contest 21

Facebook 11, 111
Farsi 108, 167
Faster-Than-Light-Dance-Company 61
Faust 98

Finland/Finnish 4–9, 30, 34, 43, 54, 56, 98, 114, 123, 129–31, 133, 138, 142, 154, 156–7, 168, 173, 179–82
Finnish National Ballet 157, 167
flamenco 166
Fokine, Mikhail 120
folk dance/folk dancer 4, 6, 21–22, 30–1, 33, 41, 45–6, 52–3, 63, 66–7, 101, 120, 130, 135, 138, 140, 142, 146–7, 152, 166, 175–6, 178
Fonaroff, Nina 168
Foucault 67
France/French 46, 49, 58–9, 92, 119, 172
Frankfurt 165
Fuller, Loie 118

Gaga 43–4
GAME 107
German Opera 51
Germany/German/West Germany/East Germany 1, 7, 9–10, 23, 25, 32, 46, 54–5, 79, 99, 107–8, 131, 137, 142, 144–5, 155, 159, 167, 170, 179, 181
Ghana 93
Giselle 153
Graham, Martha 49–50, 74, 168
Greece 122, 138
Grigorovich, Yury 49, 89
Grotesque theatre 56
Grundtvig, Niels Frederik Severin 110

Havana 170
Helsinki 4, 6, 13, 15, 28, 36, 43, 45, 54, 56, 82, 91–4, 98, 109–10, 113–15, 129–31, 134, 144, 149, 157, 167–71, 173, 175, 179–80, 182, 183
hip-hop 28, 43, 94, 127, 139, 149, 157, 178
Højskole 110
Holland 165
Home 171

Inao, Yoshifumi 43
Inger, Johan 104
Iran/Iranian 107, 144, 151, 167, 170, 179
Iranian Revolution 28

Iraq 99, 115
Ireland 95
Irish dancing 171

Jackson, Michael 27
Japan 23, 104, 124, 153, 162, 181
jazz ballet 50, 168
jazz dance 23, 111, 172
jazz music 63
Jurgów i Góralski 78

Kenyans 93
Kill Bill 23
Kinshasa 126
Krakowiak 27
Kreuzberg 151
Kylian, Jiri 66, 68, 126

La Sylphide 21
Laguna, Ana 64
Lapland 95, 173
Larbi Cherkaoui, Sidi 83, 124
Last Samurai, The 23
Latin/Latina/Latino 30, 54, 109
Latvia/Latvian 6–9, 36, 52, 92, 126, 141, 147, 150, 172
Lee, Bruce 22
Leningrad 145
Lithuania 6–9, 43, 45, 47, 63, 88, 140, 178
London 51, 60–1, 105, 114, 163, 168, 170–1
London Contemporary Dance School 60, 168
Los Angeles 171
Lublin 27
Lund 35, 56, 71, 96, 117, 121–2, 131, 173
Luther, Bill 91
Lutheran tradition 142

Madagascar/Madagasi 45, 91–2, 129, 144, 179
Malmö 23, 25, 27, 32, 43, 59, 68, 77, 81, 97–8, 103, 106, 111, 114, 121, 129, 135, 140, 156, 167, 171
Malmö City Theatre Company 77
Martha Graham School 50

Martin, Dean 81
Maximova, Ekaterina 119
Mazowsze Dance Ensemble 31
mazurka 34
Mercury, Freddy 27
miloga 71
Minus 7 81
Moiseyev, Igor 133
Moiseyev Dance Company/Moiseyev Dance School 41–2, 53, 133, 160
Montano, Linda 168
Mörköooppera 4
Moscow 19, 38, 41, 49, 53, 55, 58, 74, 118, 128, 133, 160, 180
Mother 75
Moulin Rouge 167
Muldoom, Royston 50, 159, 161
Muonio 34
Muslim 39
Myth 125

Næstved Asylcenter 107
Naharin, Ohad 43
Napoli 77
Neukolln 1
Neumeier, John 86
Nevsky Prospect 14, 30
New York 78, 162, 164–5, 168, 172
New Zealand 14–15, 67, 79, 111, 163
Nijinsky, Vaslav 120
Nirvana 27
No fixed points 74
North America 172
Nureyev, Rudolf 50, 52

Olos 34
On tradition 99
Open Look Dance Festival 72–3
Oracle 78–9
Osa 27
Oslo 44
Oulu 37–8, 66, 72, 95–6, 117, 120, 130, 133
Oxford 32

Pakistani 99
Palestine 156

Paris 49, 58, 74, 92, 134, 167
Pegida 144, 182
Petipa, Marius 118
Pineapple Dance Studio 163
Plisetskaya, Maya 119–20
Podhale 78
Poland 7–9, 14, 21, 41, 46, 59, 68, 78, 84, 89, 126, 138, 140, 162, 166–7, 177
Polish Dance Theatre 41, 125, 154
Polish National Ballet 84, 162
polka 34
polonaise 96
Poznań 9, 24, 41, 43, 65–6, 89, 105, 125, 139, 153, 161, 166, 177, 178
Preljocaj, Angelin 49, 58

Rambert Dance School 51, 54
Red Cross 88, 107
Rhythm is it 159
Riga 30, 33, 36, 52, 54, 56, 58, 92, 94, 100, 103, 126, 134, 141, 146, 150, 170, 172
Rovaniemi 21–2, 31, 34, 38, 41, 46, 63, 67, 70, 76, 82–3, 86, 95, 123, 136, 152, 173
Royal Swedish Ballet/Royal Swedish Ballet School 104, 156, 162, 167
rumba 21, 154, 170
Russia/Russian 4, 6–10, 15, 28, 41, 49, 53, 55, 57–8, 73–4, 92, 114, 118, 131, 143, 145, 148, 160, 165, 167, 170–1, 180
Rwanda Tribunal 129

Saariselkä 34
Sacre du Printemps 111, 159
Sahara 82
salsa 21, 30, 35, 54, 96, 154, 171
samba 21, 171
Santa Claus 95, 136
Satumaa 142
Saturday Dance Nights 138
Sevilla 166
Siberia 167
Sietuva Dance Company 45

Slavic spirit 126
Sleeping Beauty 49
Snow White 46
Somewhere Over The Rainbow 81
Song and Dance Celebration 134
Sorbonne 49, 58, 59
South America 162
Soviet Union 9, 10, 24, 133, 138, 141, 145, 149
Spain 166
Spisz 78
St Petersburg 13–15, 30, 35, 39, 56–7, 70, 72, 74, 96, 102, 131, 133–4, 143, 145–6, 148, 165
St Petersburg Art Residency 146
Stanislavski 56
Stockholm 8, 22, 27, 64, 79, 83, 90–1, 103, 111, 124, 127, 153, 157, 162, 164, 167, 171, 177, 181
Stravinsky 27
Sundsvall 3
Sutra 83
Swan Lake 21, 26, 38, 49, 104, 153
Sway 81
Sweden 6–9, 121, 153, 162, 164–5, 173–4, 181
Syria 115, 155, 179

Tampere Conservatory 152
Tango 5, 34–5, 71, 96, 117, 122, 131–2, 138, 142, 160
Tanzania 94, 129
Tehran 28, 167, 170, 179
Tel Aviv 44, 151
Tokyo 22, 153
Touch Compass 67
Trinity Laban Conservatoire of Music and Dance 168
Turkey/Turkish 2, 99, 140

UK 170
Ukraine 141–2
Umeå 3
United States 52, 67, 72, 118–19, 162, 165, 172
Uppercut Dance Company 123, 159

Uspenski Cathedral 167
Uzbekistan 39

Vaasa 3, 5
Vaganova 6, 41
Vaskiluoto 3
Viennese Waltz 34
Vilnius 20, 23, 25–6, 40, 42–3, 45, 47–8, 50, 63, 68–9, 78, 83–4, 86, 106, 122, 125, 127, 139–40, 152, 175–6, 178
Vivaldi 27

Waltz 5, 34, 71, 138
Warsaw 9–11, 14, 21, 25, 33, 41, 65–6, 68, 80, 84, 126, 138, 140, 154, 162, 167
Weg: A-way 76
Wigman, Mary 74, 140
WordPress 74
World War I 139
World War II 2, 7–9, 41, 139
Wrocław 65

Zayas, Guillermo 154
Zumba 54